LAMP AT MIDNIGHT

By
Barrie Stavis

Fiction
HOME, SWEET HOME!
THE CHAIN OF COMMAND

Plays
COAT OF MANY COLORS
HARPERS FERRY
THE MAN WHO NEVER DIED
REFUGE

LAMP AT MIDNIGHT

A Play about Galileo

by

BARRIE STAVIS

INTRODUCTION BY
TYRONE GUTHRIE

South Brunswick
New York: A. S. Barnes and Co.
London: Thomas Yoseloff Ltd

Library of Congress Catalog Card Number: 66-19136

The photographs accompanying the text of *Lamp at Midnight*
are from the Hallmark Hall of Fame Production, produced
and directed by George Schaefer. They were taken by Declan
Haun (Black Star).

Published simultaneously in the United States and Canada

PRINTED IN THE UNITED STATES OF AMERICA

FOR BERNICE

Contents

Illustrations

Introduction

For more than twenty years, Barrie Stavis has been engaged in writing a series of four plays, a tetralogy, and in the process has developed a dramatic style of great power and individuality. His plays are social and political documents only insofar as he is grieved by man's inhumanity to man, passionate in his belief that we can, and very occasionally do, sublimate our animal ferocity and fear of what is unfamiliar to the vision of the sage, the courage of the martyr, the spirituality of the saint.

In each play the theme is the conflict between a Dedicated Man (Galileo in *Lamp at Midnight;* Joe Hill in *The Man Who Never Died;* John Brown in *Harpers Ferry;* Joseph of Egypt in *Coat of Many Colors*), the blindness and selfishness of authority and the inability of the masses to understand their own stake in the conflict. Inevitably, this theme places its author in the ranks of those who are discontented with the status quo. *Lamp at Midnight,* as well as the other three plays, is thematically and technically ahead of its time.

Let me now tell you about *Lamp at Midnight.* On a night in 1609, Galileo turned his new telescope to the heavens and there discovered the true order of our solar system. For hundreds of years, the Church had allied itself with Aristotle and his followers, who proclaimed that the earth was the center of the universe and that the sun and stars revolved around it. This decision was not lightly reached by the Church Fathers. The Aristotelian concept of a stationary earth, with the sun and stars revolving around it, was most consonant with Christian theology. But when Galileo, a devout Catholic and true son of the Mother Church, turned his telescope to the night skies, he created a multi-faceted revolution.

3

INTRODUCTION

"The sun also ariseth, and the sun goeth down, and
hasteth to the place where he arose." "Sun, stand thou still
upon Gibeon; and thou, Moon, in the valley of Ajalon.
And the sun stood still, and the moon stayed." For centuries, such statements in the Bible were taken to be
literally true and were taught as facts. For centuries,
theologians asserted that science must be made to agree
with Church doctrine, that if any phenomenon in nature
were at odds with Church doctrine, it was the duty of the
scientists to make nature conform to the Bible. If Galileo's
astronomy were true, then the statements in the Bible were
open to question; if Biblical statements were false, what
would happen to Christian teaching?

The spiritual implications of Galileo's astronomy went
further. As Cardinal Bellarmin explains to Galileo in the
play, "What will happen to the masses of men who have
been nurtured in the belief that the world was created for
man, and that he is God's especial concern? They would
feel cheated, belittled, denigrated. They would turn in
revulsion. Heresy, apostasy, atheism would be the order
of the day. You would create a spiritual revolution . . ."

Galileo also found himself in conflict with the scientists
of his day whose "scientific" activity consisted, in the main,
of interpreting Aristotle. If nature seemed to contradict
Aristotle, then by appropriate juggling, nature must be
made to agree with Aristotle's dicta. Galileo argued that,
to find the truth, the book of Nature must be read and the
facts observed and recorded. The great battle of the induc-
tive versus the deductive approach to science was fully
engaged. And Galileo's discoveries, and his skillful polem-
ics to advance them, thrust him squarely into battle
with his Church and with the philosophers and the scientists of his day, who had a vested interest in the status quo.

Galileo recanted. He recanted not out of fear, but because of love of his Church. It was only when he was a
semi-prisoner of the Inquisition, after his recantation and
a year in exile, that he arrived at the truth which served
him for the rest of his life: "I say that if a man takes away
reason to make room for revelation, he puts out the light
of both."

4

INTRODUCTION

Now it is a most difficult feat to take complex scientific and theological ideas and translate them on the stage into turbulent drama. Yet this is what Barrie Stavis has done in *Lamp at Midnight*. The play moves with fury, advancing from scene to scene at a violent pace to its inevitable conclusion. In an age where, in general, playwrights have dealt with the smaller aspects of neurotic interpersonal relationships, Barrie Stavis has steadfastly, often doggedly, pursued his own course.

Lamp at Midnight, nearly a quarter of a century old, the first of the tetralogy, is rich in characterization and dialogue, ingenious in stagecraft, felicitous in construction, and is even more contemporary than when first written. I commend this play to you!

TYRONE GUTHRIE
—January 1966

Production History

Lamp at Midnight has had numerous productions since its first presentation in New York by New Stages, Inc., on December 21, 1947. Directed by Boris Tumarin, the original cast included: Peter Capell, Kermit Murdock, Martin Balsam, Joe O'Brien, Ben Irving, Leon Janney, Willard Swire, Jay Barney, Paul Mann, Michael Howard, Dorothy Patten, Karl Weber, William Brower, Earl I. Hammond, Raymond Gordon, Frederic DeWilde, Kathryn Eames, Ralph Camargo, Ernest Stone, Earl George, Arnold Robertson, John Merlin, Terry Becker, Joseph Silver, Frank Butler, Hal Studer, Lee Sherer, Mort Neudell, Larry Robinson, Martin Tarby, Robert Davis.

The first European presentation was by the Bristol Old Vic on October 16, 1956, directed by John Moody. The members of the cast were: Peter O'Toole, Rachel Roberts, Alan Dobie, Joseph O'Conor, Robert Lang, Edward Hardwicke, Arthur Blake, Wendy Williams, John Floyd, Eric Thompson, Nicholas Brady, Alex Scott, Michael Meacham, Wendy Hutchinson, Rashid Carrapiett, Terence Scully, Alan Shellard, Trevor Williams.

Lamp at Midnight has had numerous university productions. The first was at Amherst College, January 1948, under the direction of F. Curtis Canfield. Its most recent production was at Brigham Young University, January 1965. Under the direction of Harold I. Hansen, this presentation marked the opening of the Fine Arts Center.

Barrie Stavis's play was given its television debut on the Hallmark Hall of Fame on April 27, 1966. The cast, directed by George Schaefer, included: Melvyn Douglas, Michael Hordern, David Wayne, Hurd Hatfield, Kim

7

Hunter, George Voskovec, Eric Berry, Joanna Roos, Hugh Franklin, Thayer David, Stephen Gray, Roy Scheider, Graham Jarvis, John Gerstad, Ralph Clanton, House Jameson, Ted van Griethuysen, Gaylord Cavallaro, Richard Woods, Guy Repp, George Turner, C. K. Alexander, Norman Roland, Rex Thompson, Jordan Charney, Robert Breen, Norman Barrs.

Production Notes

THE DESIGN OF THE SET. The single feature should be a series of graduated platforms and steps. In one scene a platform can be used as the workshop area, while in another it serves as the dais of the Papal Throne. The steps can be used in one scene to lead to the balcony, and in another be the ascending benches in the Church. Also, two scenes at opposite ends of the stage can be played against each other in counterpoint, and then blend when a character from one scene walks across the stage and moves into the other scene. The simplicity of the set will provide fluidity and enrich the action by allowing it to flow continuously.

LIGHTING. Lighting plays an important part in the production of this work; it will serve to spot one part of the stage when the other is not in use. Lighting will, where needed, instantly change the setting from one scene to another. It is further suggested that light and space in the first scenes of the play should express the earlier freedom and success of Galileo; in later scenes, those of Galileo's travail, light and space should be contracted, thus suggesting the gradual and tragic limiting of Galileo's freedom.

Cast of Characters

(in order of appearance)

Galileo Galilei

Polissena, later Sister Maria
   Celeste

Sagredo Niccolini

Gepe Mazzolini

Magini

Sizzi

Libri

D'Elci

Prince Cesi

Fabricius

Terenzio

Cesare

Count Morosini

Cardinal Zacchia

Cardinal Maffeo Barberini,
   later Pope Urban VIII

Aldobrandini

Bishop of Viesta

Archbishop of Naples

Ambassador Viglienna

Cardinal Bellarmin

Father Clavius

Cardinal Verospi

Carlo Barberini

Francesco Barberini

The Major Domo

Venetti

Landini

Page

Father Firenzuola

Father Riccardi

Monsignor Ciampoli

Attendant

Three Inquisitors

Cardinal Borgia

Mother Superior

Cardinals, Guards, Clerks, Pages, etc.

"I say that if a man takes away reason to make room for revelation, he puts out the light of both."

LAMP AT MIDNIGHT

The action of the play takes place

IN FLORENCE:

Galileo Galilei's Workshop and Laboratory
The Convent of St. Matthew, in Arcetri, near Florence
Landini's Bookshop

IN ROME:

The Academy of the Lynx
The Terrace of Ambassador Sagredo Niccolini's
    Palace
The Vatican
The Palace of the Inquisition

TIME

Act I: 1609 to 1616

Act II: 1623 to 1633

Act III: 1633 to 1634

ACT I

Scene 1

Galileo Galilei's workshop and laboratory in Florence in the year 1609. Night time. Oil lamps and instruments are placed around the tables. Galileo is grinding a lens. Gepe, lively, about eighteen years old, Galileo's workman, is joining the barrel of a telescope to its base. Sagredo Niccolini, Florence's Ambassador to Rome and friend of Galileo, watches the proceedings with deep interest. When Gepe needs help, Sagredo quickly goes to his assistance. Polissena, Galileo's daughter, an appealing child of thirteen, is playing on a lute and singing. Galileo is about forty-five, has reddish hair and beard. He is given to quick, decisive motion; he has flashing eyes; his hands are expressive and dextrous. He has a hasty but well controlled temper; he is a joyous, robust man.

POLISSENA. (*Accompanying herself on the lute.*)
    "A Pilgrim poor to Zita came one day,
    And for a little water he did pray—
    'I wish, my brother, I could give thee wine,
    But if the water please thee, that is thine!'
(*She falters, having forgotten the next line. Sagredo comes to her assistance.*)
POLISSENA and SAGREDO.
    "This said, she drew the water from the well.
    And with a cross the pitcher did she sign.

15

POLISSENA. (*Alone.*)

> " 'Oh, Lord,' she said, while low her sweet
> voice fell,
> 'Make Thou this water sweet for one of
> Thine.'
> The Pilgrim drank, then astonished raised his
> head,
> 'But truly this is precious wine,' he said."

(*Galileo has taken a bit of food from a nearby plate and feeds himself with one hand while grinding with the other.*)

GEPE. (*Scolding affectionately.*) Messer Galileo, you wear yourself out. You work as though you were three people—day and night, work—work!

POLISSENA. Father! This way of eating is no good. (*Galileo draws Polissena's head close to his face. She pulls away, teasing.*) Your beard needs trimming.

(*With Sagredo's assistance, Gepe places the telescope on the stand and tightens several bolts.*)

GALILEO. Now put the large strap around the barrel. (*He watches carefully, stretching his cramped fingers.*)

GEPE. (*Working with Sagredo, but still scolding affectionately.*) When do you rest? You don't! When do you sleep? You don't! (*The bolts are tightened. Gepe presses his weight against the stand.*) Look, Messer Galileo, strong as a rock and sturdy. (*Sagredo is about to pick up the lens.*)

GALILEO. (*Cries out quickly.*) Don't! Don't touch it! Please!

SAGREDO. The grinding is finished, isn't it?

GALILEO. Yes. I'll polish as soon as this damnable cramp goes out of my fingers.

(*During the following, Galileo massages his fingers, then polishes the lens; meanwhile Polissena dozes off.*)

SAGREDO. Have you rewritten that letter to Prince Cesi of the Lynx?

GALILEO. (*Pointing to it.*) Yes. I've followed your suggestions. (*Sagredo picks it up.*) The first part is exactly as it was before. Start with the second paragraph.

SAGREDO. (*Reading from the letter.*) "And now I have a special piece of news. Several months ago I heard of a spyglass that made distant objects appear quite near. For instance, a man two miles away could be seen quite plainly. I finally succeeded in making a glass superior to the original—for my telescope reduces distance by ten."

GEPE. (*Exuberantly.*) Every square, every lane, every house—one hears nothing but talk of Messer Galileo and his spyglass—Messer Galileo and his magic box—Messer Galileo and his optic tube! The naked eye sees nothing —a Galileo tube applied to the eye, and there of a sudden stands the object. A miracle, that's what people call it. Who knows—maybe the Holy Father in Rome will canonize you. St. Galileo!

SAGREDO. (*Pats barrel of the telescope.*) A dead thing. A hollow tube of lead. A pair of lenses inserted by Galileo and it takes on life. God extracted a rib— Galileo inserted a lens. If I were a heretic, I'd say that Galileo excelled God—but being a true son of our Mother Church, I'll leave it unsaid.

GALILEO. (*Who has been enjoying it all.*) Go on— read!

SAGREDO. (*Reading from the letter.*) "Now, I am working on a new lens—even more powerful. . . . This glass of mine has many uses, and from time to time I will write, giving you news of developments."

GALILEO. And the conclusion is as I had it before.

SAGREDO. Very good. Let's send this off to Prince Cesi at once.

GEPE. (*Testing the telescope for free swinging.*) There's not a hair's variation from the diagram.

GALILEO. (*Goes over to test it. Gepe slumps wearily into a seat.*) You're tired?

GEPE. I'm one man—not three. No one has your strength.

GALILEO. I wanted the frame completed by tonight when I finish this lens.

GEPE. But you can't use it during the night! What can one see in the dark?

GALILEO. (*There is a private smile on his face.*) Go home. Rest.

GEPE. (*Putting on his coat.*) I meant to ask you, what magnification will this new lens have?

GALILEO. (*Matter-of-factly.*) Twenty diameters.

GEPE. (*Startled.*) Twenty diameters! That would bring the object closer by four hundred times. Four hundred! Messer Galileo, you *are* joking, aren't you?

GALILEO. No.

GEPE. Then something four hundred miles off will seem only a mile away!

GALILEO. If my calculations are correct.

SAGREDO. (*Attentive.*) And something forty thousand miles off would look only one hundred miles away.

GALILEO. True.

GEPE. Forty thousand miles! There is nothing on earth forty thousand miles away! The earth is round! Columbus proved it! Magellan sailed around it! (*With one hand he pantomimes the curve of the globe, with the other the straight line going off into space.*) Forty thousand miles in a straight line would be looking off into —into the sky! (*Overwhelmed.*) Into space! (*Almost frightened.*) Forty thousand miles!—Galileo! (*He flees up the steps and disappears.*)

SAGREDO. A mere man piercing through forty thousand miles. What do you think you'll see? (*Galileo turns a lamp high and studies the lens in its light. He breathes on it, then gives it a last polish. Eagerly he inserts the lens.*)

GALILEO. (*Quietly as he works.*) Call Gepe. . . . Tell him to wait for you.

SAGREDO. (*Goes to the steps.*) You don't want me to stay? Hallooo—Gepe. Wait. . . . (*A faint response.*) You will not only be looking off into space—you will be looking *at* something. At stars!

GALILEO. I know.

SAGREDO. And you will see them larger and closer than any man has ever seen them.

GALILEO. I may also see *new* stars.

SAGREDO. *New* stars?

GALILEO. Not new stars. They've been there all the time. But stars that no human eye has ever looked at.

SAGREDO. Galileo!

GALILEO. When the sky is veiled with mist we see few stars—when the night is luminous we see a multitude. My telescope will tear the veil and reveal— Gepe is waiting for you.

SAGREDO. (*With deep affection.*) Good night, my friend. (*Sagredo goes. Galileo, alone, finishes his final lens adjustment. He turns his face and looks up at the sky. A cloud passes over the moon and throws slight darkness. The cloud sails on and Galileo's face is lit with a blue-silver light. Galileo points the barrel skyward and peers into the eye-piece. He cries out in wonder and fear. He draws back and crosses himself; he has glimpsed the glory of the heavens. He peers into the telescope again as there is a sharp*)

BLACKOUT

19

ACT I

Scene 2

The light comes up immediately. The scene is the same. Galileo is standing before four seated men whom he has been addressing. They are: Professor D'Elci, Dean of the University of Pisa—a conservative academician; Professor Magini, Chief Mathematician at the University of Bologna—a pompous classicist; Professor Libri, Professor of Philosophy at the University of Pisa—a timid university man; Professor Sizzi, Florence's great astronomer—a monk, dressed in his habit. Sagredo and Polissena are present.

MAGINI. You insist that four moons revolve around the planet Jupiter?
GALILEO. I do.
MAGINI. That means that you want to increase the number of planets from seven to eleven?
GALILEO. I have nothing to do with diminishing or increasing their number! I've fastened my telescope on Jupiter night after night and I have discovered that just as our earth has one moon, so Jupiter has four moons revolving around her. *This* night I want you to look through that telescope and see them for yourself.
SIZZI. But Aristotle teaches that there are seven planets.
GALILEO. Aristotle died two thousand years ago! He knew much—but not everything. He might have been wrong.

20

LIBRI. (*Horrified.*) Aristotle wrong?

MAGINI. Are you denying his wisdom?

GALILEO. To say that two thousand years ago one man knew everything there was to know is to deny the future of mankind! Who dares set bounds to man's understanding? Who dares assume that everything that can be known in the world is already found out?

SIZZI. There are only seven planets in the sky! Aristotle said so! I'll show you the page! (*He takes a large book from Libri, who has brought it with him, and turns the pages to find the place.*)

MAGINI. (*Looking over Sizzi's shoulders.*) There!

D'ELCI. (*Looking over Sizzi's and Magini's shoulders.*) There! (*Triumphantly they hold the book open before Galileo.*)

GALILEO. (*Shutting the book without looking at it.*) What will you say when you look through this telescope and see eleven planets—with your own eyes?

MAGINI. Then I would not believe my eyes. Their existence is contrary to the principles of common sense.

SIZZI. I don't need to look. Seven! Seven! No more—no less! Aristotle said it!

GALILEO. If all science were contained in Aristotle you would be the greatest scientist in the world—you have every passage at your fingertips.

MAGINI. (*Patiently.*) But, Galileo, the world is founded on the number seven.

D'ELCI. And seven is a *holy* number.

GALILEO. For the mathematician every number is holy—none more so than any other.

MAGINI. Both nature and Scripture show that seven is holy. The seven metals of the earth. The seven golden candlesticks of the Apocalypse. The seven intervals in the octave of music.

21

SIZZI. The seven mortal sins. The seven churches of Asia. The seven penitential Psalms.

D'ELCI. And the seven days of the week named after the seven planets. Increase the number of planets and the whole system falls to the ground. Are we to have eleven days to the week? Eleven days to the week!

SIZZI. How many windows are there in the head? Seven! Two nostrils, two eyes, two ears and one mouth. So in the heavens, two favorable stars, two unfavorable, two luminaries, and Mercury, undecided and indifferent.

D'ELCI. (*Sagely.*) Seven is undoubtedly a holy number.

GALILEO. Your arguments, gentlemen, are very weighty. Had I heard them beforehand, their beautiful logic would have made me acknowledge that only seven planets could exist. But *once having seen these planets with my own eyes,* I do not consider any argument sufficiently weighty to wipe them out of the sky.

SAGREDO. Galileo put them up there with his own hands to embarrass the Aristotelians. Why don't you gentlemen turn about and embarrass him by chasing them out of the sky with a magic spell?

SIZZI. (*To Magini and D'Elci.*) I reason that even if these planets were to exist, they are invisible to the naked eye, and therefore can have no influence on the earth (*Triumphantly.*)—and therefore do not exist.

SAGREDO. Look how this great astronomer wipes out stars, by declaring them non-existent!

SIZZI. (*To Galileo.*) You've wasted our time asking us to come here. They don't exist! And even if they do, they don't. (*Magini and D'Elci nod in agreement. Libri, puzzled, is off to one side.*)

SAGREDO. (*Points to the moon, which has just risen.*)

22

And now the moon stands clear above the top of the hills! (*Looks upon the group.*) D'Elci, Dean of the University of Pisa; Magini, the great mathematician of Bologna; Libri, the great philosopher of Pisa; Sizzi, the great astronomer of Florence—which of you four will be the first to look through that telescope and confirm Galileo's observations?

GALILEO. (*Urgently, as they all hang back.*) We've fought bitterly about the two systems of the universe. You've held with Aristotle that the earth is the center of the world, and that the sun is only one of several planets revolving around the earth. I've been a disciple of Copernicus, and we say that the sun is the center of the world, and that our earth is a planet like the others, revolving around the sun. Every discovery of mine tends to confirm that our earth is a planet. Is it not possible that the entire system—stars, planets, earth, moon —is bound together by one noble law and that we stand at the edge, that it is in our power to grasp this law? That's why I've implored you to come here tonight. Eager, open-minded, young students from all Europe attend your lectures. You can spread the news of these discoveries from one end of Europe to the other! (*Pleading with them.*) Gentlemen!

SIZZI. You're very anxious to have us look through your contraption! Did you paint your celestial novelties on the inside of the barrel?

GALILEO. I'm a mathematician! (*With anger, as he points to the telescope.*) Take it apart! Ten thousand in gold if you find anything!

SIZZI. I tell you, Galileo, this moving earth of yours, this stationary sun, goes against nature and the Bible. You're preaching heresy!

GALILEO. (*Quietly.*) You have no right to use the

word "heresy."—You have no right to drag in Scripture to support your shaky prejudice. I warn you, Sizzi! You, Magini, look and be convinced.

MAGINI. (*He takes Galileo by the hand, sits him down and seats himself close by. Pompously, as if he were addressing an unreasonable and backward student.*) Let us sit down quietly and reason this out. If the earth travels around the sun, as you say, it must travel at many miles per hour, isn't that so? (*Galileo nods impatiently.*) I will give you simple proof! (*To Libri.*) Libri, you stand here. (*He places Libri in the center of the room.*) Libri is the sun. I, Magini, am the earth. I rotate around Libri. (*He begins to trot, circling slowly around Libri. A heavy man, he quickly loses his wind and talks in gasps.*) I am now going about four miles an hour—I increase my speed—five miles an hour —I now feel an increase of wind—six miles an hour! More wind! Now if I were the earth instead of myself and went at goodness knows how many miles per minute, there would be a constant gale from east to west. Buildings would fly off! Men would need claws like cats to hold on to the earth. (*Holds out his hands—still running.*) Have I claws like a cat?

D'ELCI. No, no, Magini, you're doing it incorrectly.

MAGINI. Am I? How then?

D'ELCI. According to Copernicus, the earth has double motion!—one for the day and one for the year! (*D'Elci trots alongside Magini and gives him a spin so that Magini imitates the earth's diurnal and annual rotation.*) Double motion! Double motion!

MAGINI. (*Laughing, trotting, spinning.*) Double motion! (*Magini, still moving, develops his argument.*) If the earth moved, no bird could fly to the east. The minute he rose from a branch, the tree would be carried more rapidly to the east than the bird could fly; therefore, the flight would always be to the west. And I per-

24

sonally have seen birds fly to the east. Therefore the earth is stationary, and the sun moves around it. (*Suddenly dizzy, he falls into a seat. Mopping himself, he thinks of another experiment and springs up.*) More proof! (*He places his handkerchief on the floor and steps on it.*) I shall raise myself from the ground. If the earth moves to the east I shall land against the west wall. If the earth is stationary, I will land right on this square of linen. (*He jumps up laboriously and lands on his handkerchief. Triumphantly.*) Now are you convinced?

GALILEO. Do you want to find out if I'm right, or wrong? Look through that telescope for one hour—then decide.

D'ELCI. (*To the other three.*) Gentlemen, it's getting late, shall we go? (*To Galileo.*) As Dean of the University of Pisa, I pass on the curriculum. A grave responsibility. I shall forbid not only the teaching, but even the mention of your wild speculations.

SAGREDO. Do you think your wretched silence will throw this into oblivion? You can only delay—not destroy. This new astronomy is greater than you—greater even than Galileo.

D'ELCI. (*Formally.*) Gentlemen—let us bid our host good night.

SAGREDO. (*With passion, pointing to Galileo.*) Were he himself to deny his own discoveries, offer the most ingenious and plausible arguments against them—they would still be true. This truth, once known, has a life of its own.

D'ELCI. (*Sizzi and Magini have joined D'Elci at the door. Libri has remained.*) Libri?

LIBRI. I'll stay.

D'ELCI. (*Frigidly.*) As you wish.

GALILEO. (*Sadly.*) Good night, gentlemen. (*They go. Galileo gestures hopefully to the telescope.*) Libri?

LIBRI. Aristotle is my life—I teach him in my class. You're asking me to turn my back on my whole life.
GALILEO. A life wasted teaching the lie.
LIBRI. My new term begins in three weeks. I enter the lecture hall, mount the platform and look down at those faces. I draw a breath and open my mouth for the first word. Galileo—what am I to say?
GALILEO. (*Sympathetically.*) My poor Libri.
LIBRI. Do you want me to destroy the authority of teachers and of institutions?
GALILEO. Would you rather I destroy the telescope? There are wastelands of space out there, and wastelands of man's intelligence waiting to be explored and conquered. Join with me! We stand at the edge of new worlds. We can break new ground.
LIBRI. But, Galileo, here in this book— (*Pointing to Aristotle's book, which he has in his hand.*)
GALILEO. (*Tossing the book with impatience on the table.*) My telescope forces us to write new books. What do you think I have been doing here? Taking notes—making charts—(*He points to them.*) preparing myself! A new book, Libri, on the new astronomy. You can help me.
SAGREDO. (*Taking Libri by the arm.*) One short look and you'll come back for more. It won't hurt you. I've done it more than once, and my health is excellent. (*He has casually drawn Libri before the telescope.*)
LIBRI. (*Stares at it fascinated—then.*) If I look and see — No! Leave me with what I have! (*He runs out, leaving his book of Aristotle behind.*)
SAGREDO. (*Holding the book in his hand as though weighing it.*) The prospect of change has always frightened people. They refuse to understand that there is no permanence, that axioms are temporary, that touchstones melt in the sun, that solid ground can turn to

boiling quicksand! (*He turns and sees Galileo putting his telescope away.*) What are you doing?

GALILEO. I've no heart to wander through the sky tonight.

SAGREDO. Did you expect to convince them?

GALILEO. Something! A dent—a crack in this frightening wall. . . . When are you going back to Rome?

SAGREDO. Tomorrow.

GALILEO. I'm going with you.

SAGREDO. What for?

GALILEO. I'm going to Rome to show my findings to the Church, to get the weight of Church authority behind me.

SAGREDO. The weight of Church authority?

GALILEO. Sagredo, that glorious day is soon to come when our Church becomes the open champion of new truth and knowledge.

SAGREDO. Stay away from Rome.

GALILEO. The Church herself, the College of Cardinals, the Bishops, will see the new planets, see the phases of Venus, the mountains of the moon. They will give me the stamp of their approval, because they will see with their own eyes—and with their authority behind me, I shall conquer the doubts of the timid!

SAGREDO. The sky has always belonged to the theologians. They will resent your invasion. I will not let you go to Rome and force the issue.

GALILEO. I believe in the power of logic and reason. I believe in truth. I will talk. Rome will listen and understand.

SAGREDO. And Polissena?

GALILEO. (*Polissena has come to his side.*) She is entering the convent of St. Matthew. She had planned to wait another year. But now— (*He stops, puzzled.*)

POLISSENA. But now I see that I must do it immedi-

27

ately. (*They look at each other; they have understanding.*)

GALILEO. So, Sagredo. I'm going to Rome. Will you help me or will you stand aside?

SAGREDO. I have no choice. Yes, I'll help. We'll work through the Academy of the Lynx. I will see that your membership is approved. The Lynx will arrange and advise. Perhaps, perhaps, if we handle this brilliantly enough, we may succeed.

GALILEO. Well, then—to the Lynx!

(*Polissena moves off the stage as Galileo and Sagredo move into the next scene.*)

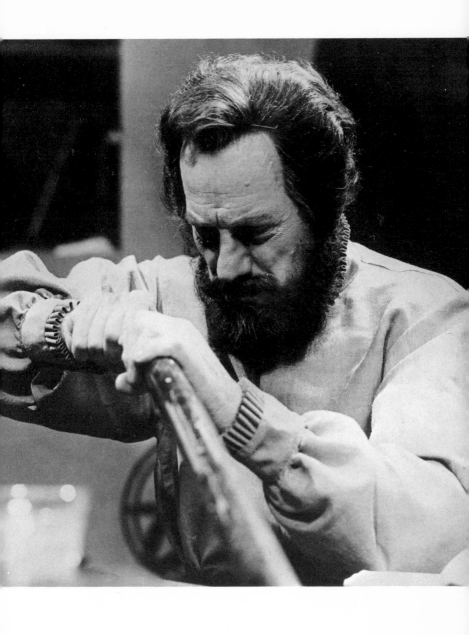

ACT I

Scene 3

The meeting of the Academy of the Lynx. Prince Federigo Cesi is concluding his speech of welcome to Galileo.

CESI. And it is with deep pride and pleasure that I invite you to sign the Book of Members of the Academy of the Lynx. (*Page brings the book, with quill and ink, before Galileo. There is an expectant hush as Galileo lifts the quill and dips it into the ink.*)
GALILEO. Where shall I sign?
CESI. (*Turns the page.*) It is our custom to give a fresh page to each member.
GALILEO. (*Gravely, but with an undercurrent of joy.*) It is no light matter, my signing this page. To join the Lynx, whose members have made so many contributions to science, is at once an honor and an obligation. But even before this Academy was formed, before any man here was born, there were other men who formed earlier societies devoted to the spirit of inquiry. By signing this page I affirm and share in the continuing history of man's genius, man's imagination, man's strength. (*Applause.*) But it is not the work I have done which I lay at your feet. Let this, my signature, be as a promise that with the instrument which God has put into my hands I will search out the truth—and set it down in a book. I shall give this book to the Lynx as my contribution to our ultimate victory over ignorance and darkness. (*Signs.*)

29

CESI. Dear Galileo, it is to the everlasting glory of the Lynx that your name is written here. (*Proudly shows Galileo's signature to members of the Lynx.*)

FABRICIUS. Let us drink a toast to Galileo.

TERENZIO. And to his telescope!

FABRICIUS. And to his book on the new astronomy.

CESARE. To the freedom of science, and to the freedom of thought!

CESI. (*Signals to the Page, who passes the wine which has already been poured into cups. Count Morosini comes in quickly. He is excited. The moment he enters everyone turns to him.*) Ah, Count Morosini. What's the news?

MOROSINI. Only the best. The gathering will be in your villa, Sagredo, and after the wine and fruit and amiable conversation, the guests will be invited out on the terrace—(*To Galileo.*)—where your telescopes will be waiting for them.

CESI. Will they all come?

MOROSINI. Flood, fire and pestilence—they'll come. Here is a list. The important ones have accepted. The others will be afraid to stay away.

SAGREDO. (*After a quick look.*) Excellent! (*Several people crowd around his shoulders. There are jubilant expressions.*) Cardinal Bellarmin—isn't he coming?

MOROSINI. He may.

SAGREDO. We must do what we can to make him come.

CESARE. Cardinal Bellarmin is your man.

GALILEO. But who is—? I don't seem to recall exactly—?

FABRICIUS. The greatest theologian since St. Thomas Aquinas.

CESARE. Incorruptible!

MOROSINI. While other men enter the Church and build their family fortune, he has refused the Papacy.

GALILEO. Refused the Papacy? Why?

MOROSINI. To leave him free of all administrative duties but one.

GALILEO. And that—?

MOROSINI. His duties in the Inquisition.

FABRICIUS. He has one guiding passion—the salvation of Christian souls.

SAGREDO. Through the Inquisition he has the power to reach out and force Christian salvation down a man's throat whether he wants it or not.

CESI. Come, the toast! What shall it be?

GALILEO. Since we stand at the threshold of a new world, let the toast be, "To the new world."

ALL. To the new world! (*They drink. There is general gaiety, laughter and excitement.*)

SAGREDO. (*Gradually edging Galileo to the side.*) Things aren't going too badly. We might yet succeed. Let us get down to important business. Here is the list of the people who have been invited. (*Gives him the list. His voice fades quickly as the lights dim down.*) You must memorize the names and the information I'm going to give you regarding each man. For instance, watch for Viglienna, the Spanish Ambassador— (*As Sagredo and Galileo talk on one side of stage, the lights dim down quickly on the scene. They then slowly dim down on Galileo and Sagredo, and come up meanwhile on the full stage to reveal the terrace of Sagredo's palace. Galileo and Sagredo move into the scene, followed by various members of the Lynx.*)

ACT I

Scene 4

The terrace of Sagredo's palace, situated on a hill. Rome lies stretched out before them.

This is an interlocking scene, with the action taking place on various levels, and blending as indicated. Galileo, with the aid of four of his telescopes, each of which has its own group of people clustered around it, is showing the heavens to various noblemen and church dignitaries. Two of the telescopes (groups one and two) point to the sky, the third (group three) is pointed into the audience, toward some object a mile off, the fourth (group four) is being dismantled. The first group consists of Cardinal Maffeo Barberini, who is peering at the heavens through the telescope, and Cardinal Zacchia, who cries out impatiently.

ZACCHIA. (*Of group one.*) Come away from that telescope, Barberini, and give me a chance at it.
BARBERINI. (*Of group one. Peering intently.*) Just one more minute.
ZACCHIA. One would think it were part of your anatomy.
BARBERINI. I wish it were. I'd lie on my back and do nothing but probe the skies.
ZACCHIA. Or turn your eyes earthward and probe what you should not probe.
BARBERINI. Charming thought! Earthly delights when I tired of heavenly wonders.

ZACCHIA. But it is not part of your anatomy! Let me! (*Barberini reluctantly moves aside and Zacchia pounces on the telescope.*)

GALILEO. (*To fourth group, who are dismantling the telescope and are at a loss as to how to continue.*) Your Highness must loosen this band and the lens will then slip out.

ALDOBRANDINI. (*Of group four.*) Thank you, Messer Galileo. (*Galileo moves off.*)

BISHOP OF VIESTA. (*Of group three. As he peers into the telescope pointed earthward.*) I can make out the letters of the inscription! (*He spells out the first word.*) O-M-N-I-U-M.

ARCHBISHOP OF NAPLES. (*Of group three. Impatiently.*) Let me see.

BISHOP OF VIESTA. (*Spells out two more words.*) U-R-B-I-S E-T.

ARCHBISHOP OF NAPLES. (*Frigidly.*) It is not seemly for a bishop to take precedence over an archbishop! (*Bishop of Viesta scrambles away from the eyepiece.*) Thank you. (*Archbishop of Naples stares through the telescope, enraptured.*) Amazing! As if I were standing before the building!

GALILEO. (*Approaches them.*) Look to the heavens, Your Reverences. You can see the buildings of Rome with the naked eye.

ARCHBISHOP OF NAPLES. If one can read this inscription and then with the same instrument observe your moon and planets there is no possibility of trickery. We will proceed in our own fashion.

GALILEO. (*Withdrawing.*) Very well, Your Reverences.

BARBERINI. (*Who has been working his way to Galileo. Now they come face to face.*) My congratulations! Everything exactly as you've said.

GALILEO. Thank you, Cardinal Barberini.

33

BARBERINI. And yet—even as I admire Jupiter and her moons, this host of extravagant heavenly beauty, I cannot help but wonder how you will make this astronomy of yours fit in with Holy Scripture.

GALILEO. I do not anticipate any great difficulty.

BARBERINI. How so? Or do you intend to advance a doctrine of double truth?

GALILEO. A doctrine of double truth?

BARBERINI. Two contradicting truths, existing side by side—one religious, the other scientific. Each valid in its *own* category, but false in the other.

GALILEO. Such theological juggling bewilders me.

BARBERINI. It's really very simple once you get the knack of it. (*They laugh.*)

VIGLIENNA. (*Of group two. Calling out.*) Messer Galileo, will you point it to Venus?

GALILEO. Gladly. (*To Barberini, as they move over to the second telescope.*) I brought six of my telescopes. I see that I should have brought six times six.

BARBERINI. And even that would hardly be enough. . . . Where are the other two?

GALILEO. One is at the Academy of the Lynx.

BARBERINI. Did you know that I am a member of the Lynx?

GALILEO. But I did not see you at the meeting.

BARBERINI. Religious duties. And where is the other telescope?

GALILEO. It is at the Roman College where the Jesuits are making independent observations. (*He directs the telescope to Venus. Silence as Galileo adjusts the telescope. The lights on this part of the stage dim down and the characters freeze in their positions. Meanwhile lights come up on another part, a higher level, and reveal Cardinal Robert Bellarmin addressing Father Clavius and three other members of the Roman College.*)

BELLARMIN. Brothers in Christ, let me have your

serious opinion on the following points: Do you approve that there exist great numbers of fixed stars invisible to the naked eye but which can be seen by means of a telescope? Do you approve that Venus is subject to changing phases similar to those of the moon? Do you approve that the surface of the moon is irregular and uneven? Do you approve that the planet Jupiter has grouped around her four mobile stars?

CLAVIUS. Cardinal Bellarmin, you have prefaced each of your questions with the word "approve." Will you kindly enlighten us on the meaning of the word "approve"? Has it scientific or theologic connotation?

BELLARMIN. I have used the word advisedly. The connotation is religious. As scientific authorities of the Roman College, you may give me purely scientific answers. As for myself—as a member of the Holy Inquisition, pure science cannot exist. Your statement must be taken and transmuted theologically. (*The lights go down on the four members of the Roman College while a sharp light picks up Bellarmin, who moves to a robed and cowled Dominican.*) Clerk of the Inquisition, open up a file for one Galileo Galilei, an astronomer. Let it be looked into if he has ever had any dealings with anyone accused of heresy. (*The light on this section of the stage fades completely and comes up sharply on the scene of the terrace as before. The characters unfreeze.*)

ALDOBRANDINI. (*Of group four. To Cardinal Verospi, who is shaking the hollow barrel of the dismantled telescope.*) Be careful! Something might fall out!

VEROSPI. (*Of group four.*) So much the better! That's what we're trying to do. (*Shakes it violently, then peers into it.*)

ALDOBRANDINI. Do you see anything? A planet or two artfully contrived on the inside? (*Aldobrandini peers into the other end. Then they lower the telescope and face each other. Aldobrandini shaking it again, still*) *not believing.*) Nothing! Nothing at all! Only lenses and a hollow tube of lead!

VEROSPI. Now let us put it together and look at Galileo's moon. (*They begin to assemble the telescope.*)

GALILEO. (*Who has finally directed the telescope at Venus. To Viglienna.*) If it please Your Worship, it is now pointed to Venus.

VIGLIENNA. Thank you. (*He peers into the telescope.*)

BARBERINI. (*Resuming his conversation with Galileo.*) But seriously, if you don't advance a doctrine of double truth, how will you reconcile your new astronomy with Scripture?

GALILEO. As a scientist I can only report what I see.

BARBERINI. But if what you see seems to be at odds with Church Doctrine, what then, Galileo?

GALILEO. Scripture tells us how to go to heaven, but not how the heavens go.

BARBERINI. But you still haven't answered my question. If what you see is at odds with Church doctrine, *which is to take precedence?* (*Galileo is silent.*) Must the Church make Scripture agree with nature?

GALILEO. (*In a low voice.*) Yes.

BARBERINI. (*Perturbed.*) Galileo, you are treading on dangerous ground.

GALILEO. Consider. Scripture is the word of God; Nature is the deed of God. Now nature is immutable, with no variation of any kind. But the word of God is written in allegory, subject to many interpretations.

BARBERINI. That is undeniably true. So?

GALILEO. So, since there are many interpretations of the word, and only one to the deed, and since both are part of the same truth and cannot contradict each other, should not the *word* be made to conform with the deed?

BARBERINI. (*With cynical admiration.*) You reason

like a Jesuit. The Church lost a valuable servant when you turned to science.

GALILEO. You misjudge the spirit in which I speak.

BARBERINI. Undoubtedly your argument has point. Yes. Yes. But you do reason like a Jesuit.

GALILEO. Do not mock me! This opinion has come through an agony of thought!

BARBERINI. (*With warm concern.*) I see you believe what you're saying. But, Galileo, for hundreds of years theologians have asserted that science must be made to agree with Church doctrine. Now you say it should be the other way around—that with each new discovery in science, the Church reinterpret Scripture!

GALILEO. Why should the Church burden herself with conclusions which may later be proven false?

BARBERINI. I would not like to be the Pope whose duty it would be to reinterpret Scripture in the light of your astronomy—or worse, to choose between them.

GALILEO. Such a thing need never happen.

BARBERINI. (*Gravely.*) I pray not. (*At this point Bellarmin enters.*) Ah, Cardinal Bellarmin, good evening!

BELLARMIN. Good evening, Barberini. (*A number of others come forward to him. He is respected.*)

GALILEO. (*This is a most vital moment.*) Cardinal Bellarmin, will you look? (*Waves him to the telescope.*)

BELLARMIN. Thank you, my son, but I have already looked through one of your telescopes, and have had occasion to admire your more than excellent astronomy.

GALILEO. You have! But where . . . ?

BELLARMIN. At the Roman College.

GALILEO. And you have seen . . . ? (*He hangs on Bellarmin's words.*)

BELLARMIN. I have not yet decided what I have seen.

GALILEO. Not yet decided?

BELLARMIN. My son, no fact is a pure fact. The aura of attendant consequence can never be severed from the fact itself.

GALILEO. I see. (*Bellarmin moves toward one of the groups.*)

BARBERINI. (*To Galileo, as the lights begin to fade out.*) Win him over and you've won the entire Church! (*The lights dim down as Galileo moves off into the next scene.*)

ACT I

Scene 5

An office in the Palace of the Inquisition. Galileo and Bellarmin are deep in discussion. A Dominican Father, to the rear and out of focus of the scene, is busily writing.

BELLARMIN. No, Galileo, I offer you no hope. The Church cannot allow your new astronomy. Roman Catholicism is committed to the system of Aristotle.

GALILEO. But, Cardinal Bellarmin, all I ask is that the Church officially witness a scientific demonstration. In what way will that harm our Mother Church?

BELLARMIN. You still consider this a purely scientific question?

GALILEO. Is it not?

BELLARMIN. The scientific considerations are secondary.

GALILEO. How so, my Lord?

BELLARMIN. As Christianity developed, it became urgent to adopt a single official system of the universe. The Fathers of the Church found Aristotle's system most in accord with the spirit of Scripture. For hundreds of years the astronomy of Aristotle and the heavens of Christian theology have been as one! Now you come forward and say, "The old celestial hierarchy is false! I will introduce the true system!" (*Courteously.*) And perhaps it is—for I respect your scientific work and think you personally a great man.

GALILEO. Thank you. And surely Your Eminence knows in what esteem I hold him?

39

BELLARMIN. But the truth or falsity of your system is not my concern! I must ask only one question: *What will happen to Christian teaching if our system of the heavens were to be torn down and your system set up in its place?* And the answer is: *Christian truth would be destroyed!*

GALILEO. My Lord!

BELLARMIN. You would transform the Church of the entire universe into the church of one insignificant clod of dirt, lost in space. . . .

GALILEO. My Lord!

BELLARMIN. You think I exaggerate? What will happen to the masses of men who have been nurtured in the belief that the world was created for man, and that he is God's especial concern? They would feel cheated, belittled, denigrated. They would turn in revulsion. Heresy, apostasy, atheism would be the order of the day. You would create a spiritual revolution.

GALILEO. (*Stopping his ears with his hands—in deep agony.*) Cardinal Bellarmin!

BELLARMIN. (*Pulling Galileo's hands away from his ears forcefully, in sharp contrast to his normally staid and venerable motions.*) You can cry out my name—but do you think your voice imploring me to silence can change the significance of your discovery! Aristotle's heavens and the Christian heaven—the destruction of one would injure the other. This we cannot allow.

GALILEO. (*Choked.*) Oh, my Lord, you have just started a civil war inside me which will end in my destruction!

BELLARMIN. (*Graciously.*) No! No civil war and no destruction. Which do you hold more precious, your ephemeral science or your eternal Catholic soul?

GALILEO. Is *that* the choice?

BELLARMIN. What else?

40

GALILEO. No—that is not the choice. It will be to the eternal glory of the Church to be the first to acknowledge this concept. Think! Man by the power of his imagination and the reasoning of his intellect sweeping out beyond the farthest reaches of space and binding the universe into one noble law. Once able to comprehend this concept and hold it shining in his soul, man becomes a precious vessel. . . . Aristotle's system is false and mine is true!

BELLARMIN. My son, truth is a philosophic fiction! Make a declarative statement to me and I'll prove it to be lie or truth, whichever best suits the interest of our Holy Mother Church.

GALILEO. Your Eminence knows how highly I regard your theological learning.

BELLARMIN. Where the salvation of the soul is concerned, the Church teaches that there is no absolute truth. Something is true in proportion to the good or evil it does. For better or worse the Church fathers have committed us to Aristotle's astronomy. Were we to change now, the evil would be too great! Therefore there can be no change. (*With gracious comforting sympathy to Galileo.*) You've heard the admonition. You will obey and abandon your opinion?

GALILEO. (*In a low choked voice.*) I will obey.

BELLARMIN. I am pleased—otherwise it would have been necessary to proceed further. Injunction. Imprisonment.

GALILEO. Cardinal Bellarmin! The salvation of my soul is no light matter! I came to Rome to defend my Catholic name and to plead the cause of science. At no time was there any question in my mind of disobedience!

BELLARMIN. I am pleased, my son. I would have regretted using stringent measures. You are personally very dear to me. (*With consideration.*) Galileo, your enemies are spreading a false report that you are being punished by the Holy Office, forced to recant your opinions. (*Galileo is disturbed.*) To protect your rights and so that there may be no misunderstanding, I give you this memorandum which tells you what you may or may not do. Guard it well, Galileo, you may need it in the future. (*Gives it to him.*)

GALILEO. I will.

BELLARMIN. And remember—as a Catholic, your rights of opinion are limited, and this memorandum clearly defines the limitations. But within them, you are free.

GALILEO. (*Looks through it quickly—then, with hope in his voice.*) This document makes the distinction between advancing the Copernican system as hypothesis or fact?

BELLARMIN. Certainly. There has never been any question on that point.

GALILEO. I can state it as hypothesis! A reprieve!

BELLARMIN. Galileo, employ your reprieve with discretion.

GALILEO. Cardinal Bellarmin, may I ask you to explain to me the wide cleft between hypothesis and fact? Why does the Church allow the first and ban the second?

BELLARMIN. Advanced as fact, the entire masses of people would hear it. It would start a great deal of argument and speculation which could only end in harming the Church. . . . Advanced as hypothesis, who will hear of it? A few scholars here and there, who will use it mathematically as needed. And as for the masses of people, they will consider this juggling of the heavens an esoteric toy for scientists to play with.

GALILEO. But I do have the Church's permission to advance it as hypothesis?

BELLARMIN. As hypothesis, yes. The Church is willing to allow mathematicians and scientists their intellectual devices.

GALILEO. One thing more before you go.

BELLARMIN. Certainly.

GALILEO. Your Eminence, you spoke of the masses of people. You are convinced that they could not hear the truth and survive?

BELLARMIN. In my deepest soul I am sure of it! It is beneficial to guard them from precocious knowledge which will do them harm.

GALILEO. When will the people be ready for the truth?

BELLARMIN. Never.

GALILEO. Never?

BELLARMIN. Or at least, some time in the future.

GALILEO. But the future can be now!

BELLARMIN. My son, you are impatient. Do not try to hurry God's preordained will. (*He turns and goes off. Galileo moves to the other side of stage and into the next scene.*)

ACT I

Scene 6

A meeting of the Academy of the Lynx. There is an air of gloom, even despair. Sagredo presides as Chairman. Galileo, Cesi, Cardinal Maffeo Barberini and several others are present.

SAGREDO. We will now hear the report of Prince Cesi, President of the Lynx.

CESI. (*Rising, a weary man.*) Gentlemen, thirteen years ago we banded together and formed the Academy of the Lynx. We functioned soberly, waiting for a great discovery, a unique invention, which would stir popular imagination and focus it on the question of the right of science to develop independently. We waited eight years. Then the world was rocked by the sensational news of the telescope. Here was our heaven-sent opportunity. (*He sighs deeply.*) It soon became clear that to win the battle of the telescope was to win the battle of the freedom of thought. Gentlemen, this magnificent opportunity for which the Lynx was organized, this opportunity is gone. For under Cardinal Bellarmin's injunction, Galileo may treat the new astronomy only as hypothesis, not as fact. Gentlemen, we have lost. (*He sits down, dejected.*)

FABRICIUS. Not yet!

SAGREDO. We know the painful sequel to Prince Cesi's report and are aware of his deep grief. The chair will entertain a motion that we accept the report as complete.

44

CESARE. So moved.

TERENZIO. I second it.

SEVERAL OTHERS. Aye.

SAGREDO. Opposed? (*Silence.*) Unanimous.

FABRICIUS. Chairman?

SAGREDO. You have the floor.

FABRICIUS. We have lost this battle, but there will be others. Besides, we have many other things to our credit. Only this last year Cesare has published a book and Sagredo an excellent paper.

SAGREDO. Will someone relieve me of the chair? I want to participate in this discussion. Count Morosini? (*There are murmurs of assent. Morosini takes the chair. Sagredo, now sitting with the other members, raises his hand. Morosini recognizes him.*) May I speak directly to Fabricius? (*Morosini nods. Sagredo to Fabricius.*) You have mentioned Cesare's monograph. Very important—but with all due deference to Cesare, his book is completely obscure. It sits quietly on the shelves of fifty or one hundred private libraries, known to a handful of scientists, but for the rest of the world, a little esoteric.

GALILEO. Esoteric! Exactly the word Cardinal Bellarmin used!

SAGREDO. (*To Fabricius—there is anger and irony in his voice.*) My paper is on the anatomy of molluscs! Can we dramatize the right of science to present her findings, no matter what the theological consequences, with a paper entitled, "The Anatomy of the Molluscs Around Rock Formations on the Coast of Corsica"? We needed a unique and provocative issue like the telescope—and a telescope or its equivalent happens once in a millennium! It was given to us, to us in this room, to wage the battle. We have fought and we've been defeated. We've lost the battle for free thought.

CESARE. (*Is recognized. Heatedly, shouting one sentence in anger.*) We have Cardinal Bellarmin to thank

45

for this! (*He sits down. A low undertone of general assent and angry murmuring, as follows: "True," "He's wrong," "This is an insult," "Outrageous."*)

SAGREDO. (*Is recognized.*) To attribute our defeat to this or that church dignitary is to limit the horizon of this conflict. Cardinal Bellarmin indeed! If it were not he, it would be someone else within the Church.

TERENZIO. (*Jumps up angrily and addresses Sagredo directly.*) Are you implying that our Mother Church is our enemy?

SAGREDO. You have not been recognized by the chair. This is a meeting!—not a free-for-all.

TERENZIO. (*To Morosini.*) Chairman! Chairman! (*He is recognized, then points to Sagredo.*) May I address him directly?

MOROSINI. You may.

TERENZIO. *Are you implying that our Mother Church is our enemy?*

BARBERINI. Chairman. (*He is recognized. In a silky voice.*) Let me assure Ambassador Niccolini that he may speak with full freedom. When I attend a meeting of the Lynx, though I do not physically doff my ecclesiastical robes, nevertheless, I do leave theological dogma in the vestibule.

SAGREDO. I would say what I have to say were Cardinal Bellarmin himself in this room. The Church says to science, "This you may say—this you may not say." Though man's relationship to the physical world is changing day by day, the Church, in glorious isolation, will have none of it. The Church says, "I will rule science by decree." Science by decree! It is not Rome which will prove that the earth does not move. All the people in the world could not stop it from turning, nor could they stop themselves from turning with it! (*There are murmurs as follows: "Who does he think he is?", "That's right," "Chairman," "Be quiet," "No.*

46

No. He's wrong," "Hear him out," "Chairman," "How dare you.")

TERENZIO. Chairman! Chairman!

SAGREDO. I have not yet yielded the floor.

TERENZIO. He's out of order!

SAGREDO. Why will the Church have none of it? Because to accept the implications of the telescope would mean wiping out the vulgarities of Catholicism—miracle worship, relic worship, bribing God and Jesus with burning candles and bits of gold. (*Sagredo's speech is cut into with "I protest," "Silence," "Be quiet," "Let him speak," but he overrides them.*) It would mean sweeping away this welter of debasing superstition and setting up in its place conceptions more consonant with the dignity of man. (*Again his speech is cut into with: "Cardinal Bellarmin will hear of this," "Hear him out," "Blasphemy," "This is an insult," "He still has the floor." Again Sagredo overrides them.*) To whom could we entrust this noble ethic? Our present leaders? It is to their advantage to perpetuate these vulgarities. (*The meeting is out of hand. There are loud cries from the various members.*)

VARIOUS MEMBERS.

He's out of order.	Silence.
Chairman. Chairman.	Be quiet.
He's not talking to the point.	What is he saying?
	Listen to him.
He still has the floor.	Who does he think he is?
Chairman.	Firebrand.
Point of order.	He's right.
I want the floor.	Hear him out.
Scoundrel.	I protest.
Let him finish.	Outrageous.
Chairman.	Blasphemy.

47

How dare you? We are scientists, not rab-
Firebrand. ble.

(*The meeting is in an uproar. There is thumping on
the table, shouting. The Angelus rings. Suddenly the
room is in silence. All, with the exception of Sagredo,
cross themselves and pray. The silence prevails except
for the continued ringing of the bells.*)
SAGREDO. I will not pray!
BARBERINI. (*Who has not participated in the argument, but who has been very observant—to Sagredo.*)
Are you turning Protestant under our eyes?
SAGREDO. (*About to answer in fury, subsides. The
Angelus continues ringing. Everyone, including Cesi
and Galileo, is praying. Sagredo spreads his arms out
wide, and cries out.*) Brothers, our days of warfare have
begun. Black night and burnt ashes. No soul will be in
peace until this, our struggle, is resolved.
(*The lights have been dimming down. Now there is a*)

BLACKOUT

END OF ACT I

ACT II

Scene 1

The Convent of St. Matthew of Arcetri, near Florence. Galileo, Gepe and Polissena (now Sister Maria Celeste) are present. It is late afternoon. The sky is flaming with an already set sun. Galileo, finishing a mouthful, is pushing a plate away from before him.

MARIA CELESTE. You must finish the quince. I baked it especially for you.

GALILEO. But I'm no longer hungry.

MARIA CELESTE. You must. It's good for you.

GALILEO. (*Docilely.*) Yes, Sister. (*He nibbles.*)

MARIA CELESTE. I've been put in charge of the dispensary and I've made up two jars of medicine for you. (*She goes off for medicine. Galileo quickly and surreptitiously gives Gepe the rest of the quince. Gepe bolts it down. Maria Celeste returns with two small jars.*) Take this one, the large one with the label, at breakfast. It's made of dried figs, walnuts, rue and salt, mixed with honey. (*Galileo makes a face.*) And you must take it every morning, it's—

GALILEO. I know. It's good for me.

MARIA CELESTE. And this one, the small one without the label, is a salve to rub on your aching joints.

GALILEO. Without the label—internal consumption. With the label—external application. Give them to Gepe. Gepe, see that I take this wonderful medicine

49

every day. (*Gepe nods vigorously. Galileo seriously.*) You received my note?

MARIA CELESTE. This morning. Father, what does it mean now that Cardinal Barberini is our new Pope?

GALILEO. (*Enthusiastically.*) This is the dawn of a new day for science. We are entering an age of enlightenment and knowledge.

MARIA CELESTE. And will you really visit him?

GALILEO. Of course. He is my friend. Remember the verse he wrote in my honor?

MARIA CELESTE. The verse! (*She recites it.*)
"O brilliant ray, our Galileo's eye,
Stirs up the sluggards in our ancient sky,
Where blind philosophers must grope and sigh—
Our Galileo's made the planets fly!"

(*Galileo and Gepe have remembered the poem, for Gepe joins in the last two lines and Galileo chimes in on the last line. Laughter.*) When will you go, Father?

GALILEO. I start tomorrow—that is, if you've finished the manuscript.

MARIA CELESTE. You know I have. (*She goes for the manuscript.*)

GALILEO. Gepe, put it on the table. (*Gepe puts a wrapped telescope which he has been concealing on the table.*)

MARIA CELESTE. This work has brought me close to you. For seven years we have been working together. As you wrote it, I copied it. Now that it is completed, I'll feel lost without— (*She doesn't finish.*)

GALILEO. We will have other work together. (*Holding manuscript.*) Hypothesis! All set down as hypothesis . . . but now that Barberini is Pope, I can revise this manuscript—present its arguments openly—say to the world, this is true! (*Maria Celeste picks up the wrapped telescope.*) Open it!

MARIA CELESTE. (*Opening it.*) A telescope!

50

GALILEO. The telescope for the book. I take one-half of my life and give you the other to keep.

MARIA CELESTE. (*Stacks the telescope against the manuscript.*) The book is smaller, but more powerful. It will reach more people.

GALILEO. (*Gravely.*) The work of a lifetime. Fifty years of thought, study, experiment. I have done what I was born into this world to do. (*There is a pause. From a distant church, bells are heard, low and serene.*)

MARIA CELESTE. Your stars are coming out.

GALILEO. I know where they are, but I have difficulty seeing them. The world begins to close in around me. (*The thought strikes him.*) Is it possible that I may grow blind?

MARIA CELESTE. God wouldn't let you grow blind. You have seen His universe and shown it to man. The very stars will witness for you. (*Looks up to the sky.*) Beautiful stars of the night. How many of them are there, Father?

GALILEO. Many. Many. Perhaps even too great a number to count.

MARIA CELESTE. Even with your best telescope?

GALILEO. Men will come after me who will build larger telescopes and still larger ones—and even then the number of stars will not be counted—always there will be new ones to discover. The size of the universe is opening up.

MARIA CELESTE. But, Father, what is beyond the stars?

GALILEO. Space.

MARIA CELESTE. But beyond the space?

GALILEO. More stars.

MARIA CELESTE. And then more space? (*Galileo nods.*) Where is the farthest star—after you've passed all space?

GALILEO. There is no farthest star.

MARIA CELESTE. Where does it end?

GALILEO. There is no end.

MARIA CELESTE. No end? Oh, Father.

GALILEO. Do not be afraid, my darling. Only small people need fear the large truth. Must the universe be smooth, round and comfortably small for us to be happy in it? Man is not measured by the size of his habitation, but by the understanding of his soul. Let man penetrate the secrets of nature. Each new law of nature learned by man will be additional proof of the infinite greatness and infinite wisdom of God.

MARIA CELESTE. You know, sometimes I think it is possible that through understanding of Nature, a scientist can reach God just as well as a priest!

GALILEO. I cannot say for certain—but this I know: God works His miraculous will through man's highest aspirations. (*The bells are heard again.*) As soon as I rewrite the book I will rest. I will come and visit you, and we will sit here quietly on this very bench—quietly, quietly. In peace and quiet, I will sit out my autumn days. (*He rouses himself and with a burst of energy.*) But first I must go to Rome and obtain permission to rewrite the book. No longer hypothesis, fact! (*He picks up the manuscript.*) To Rome—and to my friend Maffeo Barberini, our new Pope! (*A light picks him up as he moves off into next scene.*)

ACT II

Scene 2

This is an interlocking scene. The first playing area is the antechamber of the Pope's audience room; the second is the audience room. Galileo and Sagredo are in the first area, which is brightly lit. In the second area are Pope Urban VIII, the former Cardinal Barberini; Carlo Barberini, his older brother; Carlo's son, Francesco, aged 26; and the Major Domo. The lighting in this scene is toned down and dim; the figures are visible, though not clearly. They are immobile while the scene in the first area is played.

GALILEO. (*With the manuscript in his hand.*) How can you talk like that, Sagredo? Don't you realize that at last the Church is in the right hands? Cardinal Bellarmin is dead and our own Maffeo Barberini is Pope.

SAGREDO. And so you think that our old troubles will fade and be gone. Wrong! Wrong!

GALILEO. Sagredo, I shall go in there, and with one wave of his hand our own beloved Maffeo will sweep our way clear. I will then rewrite the book as fact, not hypothesis, and the truth will be known.

SAGREDO. (*Shakes his head. With a sigh.*) God be with you in that room. For with Maffeo Barberini on Peter's throne, you will need God on your side! (*The light in this area dims down quickly as the light in the second area comes up sharply. Galileo and Sagredo freeze.*)

POPE URBAN VIII. (*To Francesco, his nephew.*) You are no longer merely a young man of the house of Barberini. You are my nephew. As Pope, I am empowered by custom and authority to give you certain opportunities.

CARLO BARBERINI. What are your plans, brother?

POPE. You, Carlo, will be the General of the Papal Army.

CARLO. Excellent.

POPE. Francesco, how old are you?

FRANCESCO. Twenty-six.

POPE. How would you like to be a Cardinal—my Cardinal nephew?

FRANCESCO. You are too kind to me!

POPE. Francesco Barberini, Cardinal of St. Lawrence of Damascus.

FRANCESCO. (*Kisses the Pope's ring.*) Uncle, we can make this a noble age, an age of light and good deeds!

POPE. What? Oh, yes—light and good deeds. (*To the Major Domo.*) Is there anything else on today's calendar?

MAJOR DOMO. Yes, Your Holiness. Galileo has an audience with you. His last before leaving Rome. I have set out the gifts you have for him. (*He brings them forward and goes toward Galileo, who hands the manuscript to Sagredo and moves forward to meet the Major Domo.*)

POPE. Six audiences in six weeks, and these presents— few men have been so unusually honored.

FRANCESCO. Uncle, may I stay and meet him?

POPE. Certainly. (*Galileo is ushered in by the Major Domo, who leaves immediately. Galileo kneels.*) Rise, my son—and my friend.

GALILEO. Your Holiness.

CARLO. Well, Galileo, still wandering around in the skies?

GALILEO. (*Smiling.*) Still wandering.

POPE. My nephew Francesco, an admirer of yours.

FRANCESCO. (*Deeply impressed.*) I have my own telescope—and I've read every word you've written.

GALILEO. I am honored.

POPE. An enthusiast.

CARLO. Well, Galileo, we must go. Good luck with your sky wandering.

FRANCESCO. (*Holding Galileo's hand in both of his.*) Messer Galileo, the future is to you. (*Carlo and Francesco go.*)

POPE. (*Smiling.*) My nephew is an idealistic young man. So you want permission to return to Florence?

GALILEO. Yes, Your Holiness.

POPE. We would like to keep you here by our side, for we have a special affection for you. But we know that your home and work are in Florence—so we will not be selfish.

GALILEO. Holy Father, before I go, grant me one petition, near and dear to me.

POPE. Name it, Galileo.

GALILEO. Repeal the decree of Cardinal Bellarmin. Allow me to deal with the system of Copernicus freely and truthfully.

POPE. (*With great concern.*) Alas! That is something we cannot grant!

GALILEO. In six weeks I have had six interviews with you. (*Falling on his knee.*) The world envies me, but even at this moment I am not to be envied.

POPE. (*Helping him up. He is deeply troubled.*) Listen, my friend. If it had depended upon us that decree would not have been passed. But once done, we will not undo it.

GALILEO. But Your Holiness is an enlightened man and understands the scientific method. Many nights we have studied the sky together and we have seen the extraordinary—

POPE. How do we know what we have seen? Man's mind is both frail and full-blown with conceit. The apparent reality is often the illusion.

GALILEO. But the orderliness, the perfect logic, the symmetry, the absolute simplicity of the Copernican system—?

POPE. Now, now, Galileo, by these very words you are limiting God's might!

GALILEO. *I*, limit God?

POPE. God is all-powerful, is He not, Galileo?

GALILEO. Undoubtedly.

POPE. Therefore all things are possible to Him. Is this not so? (*Galileo nods.*) Therefore to reason that the earth revolves around the sun because it is the easiest, most orderly way, you are of necessity limiting God to the easiest way. And this, Galileo, I am sure you do not intend to do.

GALILEO. Then there is no logic, no unity, no order, in the universe?

POPE. Perhaps there is—perhaps not.

GALILEO. And if God so desires He can on two different days achieve the same result by two totally different methods?

POPE. If something appears to happen one particular way, it is not for man to say it can happen in no other way. God is almighty and may do as He sees fit. In fact, the more difficult, complex and impossible it appears to us, the greater God's omnipotence.

GALILEO. Your Holiness is pleased to jest as he used to in the old days before he became—?

POPE. (*Cutting him off sharply.*) In matters of the faith we do not jest! Galileo, we do not approve of your attitude. In matters of faith we want learners, not critics. (*Galileo stands back aghast.*) You may not think or

56

dispute on the faith as you please. Faith is not an opinion, but a certitude! (*Galileo is stunned. Pope, courteously.*) Come, Galileo, we have prepared some presents for you. (*Leading Galileo to the table with presents.*) And most important, we give you a letter for your Duke. We would like you to read some of it aloud. And, Galileo, dear beloved friend, let this reading be a covenant between us.

GALILEO. (*Begins reading.*) "As long as Jupiter and his satellites shine in heaven, so long shall our Galileo's fame shine on earth as its eternal companion. With our fatherly affection we have long followed the career of this great man. We find in him not only literary distinction, but most perfect piety. And so that you may fully understand how dear he is to us, we give him this letter as a testament." (*The light dims down on this area and then goes dark. The Pope Urban VIII freezes. The first playing area lights up as Galileo crosses into it. Sagredo unfreezes.*) You were right, Sagredo. I asked him to acknowledge the truth, and instead he gave me presents.

SAGREDO. At last you see! At last you understand the facts. Now act on them. There is a ship sailing for England tonight. You will board it.

GALILEO. So you would have me flee. To the devil with your arrangements.

SAGREDO. Go to England where you can work in freedom. Galileo, my sweet friend, you are that lamp at midnight which can illuminate the darkness we have lived in. You are the only man alive who can break the chrysalis of two thousand dead years. And England is the only place where you will be able to do it.

GALILEO. No. My place is here. The weapons are not of my own choosing, but I shall fight it through.

SAGREDO. You may lose. Why take the risk?

GALILEO. For my Church, for my soul, for my book! They're all three bound together. (*Sagredo is impa-*

tient.) You agree with me that it's not enough to have written it. The book must be published and read. And that cannot be done if I go away to England.

SAGREDO. And why not?

GALILEO. If I were to publish in England without Rome's official license, who would read it? It would be a thing smuggled in the dark. I can get my hearing *only* with Rome's official license to print. I will bring the book to the Bureau of Censors. I will do anything they ask, cut or add or change, but *I will get their license*. And once I have it, I can spread the truth of Copernicus through the Church itself. For that I must stay here!

SAGREDO. (*Impressed in spite of himself.*) There is truth in what you say—undeniably. But I am uneasy. You're playing a dangerous game.

GALILEO. I am doing what is left for me to do. I came here hoping to have it as fact, but they will allow me only the hypothesis. Very well then, hypothesis it will be. That I still have. How is this dangerous?

SAGREDO. Oh, dear Galileo, who can stand up against your truth and your justice? Perhaps you are right and I am wrong. . . . But I confess I don't like the picture of you as a second Daniel in the lions' den.

GALILEO. My book shall convert the lions.

SAGREDO. (*Laughs.*) There's a good fight in you!

GALILEO. It's a fight that will decide the future. We will win that future! (*The light dims down quickly in this area, as Galileo moves into the next scene. There is no break in time.*)

ACT II

Scene 3

(*Landini's bookshop, in Florence. Galileo, seated on a stool, is off to one side, immersed in shadows. Landini is in conversation with Venetti, a cloth merchant.*)

VENETTI. (*Shyly.*) Messer Landini, how does one buy a book?
LANDINI. You're a merchant, Venetti. When I wish to purchase some of your excellent cloth, I inquire the price, pay you, and the cloth is mine. If you want a book, ask the price, pay me for it, and the book is yours.
VENETTI. Just like that?
LANDINI. Just like that.
VENETTI. How much is this book of Galileo's?
LANDINI. One crown.
VENETTI. And it's in Italian? (*Landini opens a copy and shows it to him.*) Twenty years ago I learned to read and write. It's come in very handy for my business. Now I can use this same Italian to read this book. (*Shyly.*) I've been told there's no greater pleasure than sitting at home reading a book.
LANDINI. Try it and see.
VENETTI. (*Pays for the book and starts off with it.*) If I like it, I'll come back and buy another. (*He goes.*)
LANDINI. Thank you very much. Good day. (*Triumphantly to Galileo.*) Well, Messer Galileo, that makes eighteen we've sold today.

59

GALILEO. Forgive an old man his foolishness, but I like to sit here quietly in the shadow and watch people come in and buy my book. Eighteen in one day. Whooo!

LANDINI. For the last ten days, I could have had no other stock but your book. We're nearly sold out. The next time an author comes to me for advice, I'll say to him, "Write masterpieces. There's a great market for them." . . . Excuse me, here comes Count Cinelli's page.

PAGE. (*An alert boy of about fifteen enters.*) Good afternoon, Messer Landini.

LANDINI. Good afternoon to you.

PAGE. (*Handing him a letter.*) From the Count.

LANDINI. (*Opens it, reads, smiles, calls off in Galileo's direction.*) Listen. "Galileo's new book has given me such unbounded pleasure that I must share my joy with others. I order three copies of the book. . . ." He wants one for his brother in Pisa, one for his nephew in Turin, one for his cousin in Milan. (*To the Page.*) Tell your master they will be sent at once.

PAGE. I will. (*Hesitates, then moves to Galileo.*) You are Messer Galileo, aren't you?

GALILEO. How did you know?

PAGE. By your picture in the front of the book.

GALILEO. Have *you* read my book?

PAGE. (*Cautiously.*) Only a few pages at a time when no one is around. The Count's copy is always at his bedside.

GALILEO. What do you think of it?

PAGE. (*Astonished.*) You really want to know? (*Galileo nods emphatically.*) Well, that Copernican system, it *is* real, isn't it? There are times when I can't tell from your book if you really believe it.

GALILEO. The Church does not allow the system as

a fact—but I will also tell you that all evidence refutes Aristotle's system.

PAGE. (*Vexed.*) You're confusing me. The Aristotle system makes no sense. Only one can be right. Why didn't you say exactly what you believe?

GALILEO. Landini, let this young man come in and read my book whenever he wants to. (*Picks up a copy of the book.*) My son, read! Read the book carefully. Think your way through to the answer. Don't be afraid to think!

(*The lights dim down to blackness, coming up meanwhile on the next scene. In the darkness, Galileo, Landini and the Page move off.*)

61

ACT II

Scene 4

Audience room in the Vatican.
Pope Urban VIII and Father Vincenzio Maccolini
Da Firenzuola are present.

POPE. (*Leafing through the book.*) I cannot believe it!
CARLO. (*Book in hand, enters in haste. He is in the uniform of a general of the Papal Army, and is followed by Francesco, now a cardinal, and by the Major Domo.*) Have you seen this book, brother?
POPE. Galileo's! (*Holds up his copy.*)
CARLO. (*Surprised.*) You have one too?
POPE. Father Firenzuola here brought me a copy. . . . Insufferable! Impossible!
CARLO. Insufferable—but not impossible. He has made us a laughing stock. We send missionaries to Japan and the new Americas—spend millions in gold, everything to extend the influence of the Church, and this one book damages our dignity, our prestige—
POPE. Prestige! Dignity! I could sell our dignity piece by piece in the public market down to the last scrap and build it up again within six months. But this book may lose us something we will never be able to recapture.
CARLO. Brother, what do you mean?
POPE. This book appeals to reason and not to faith! This book will encourage people to think! This book will teach people *how* to think!
CARLO. By my Saviour, you are right!

POPE. Once people begin thinking independently, the unity of the Church will fragment into a thousand parts. There will be no Church. And to make matters worse, he has written this book in Italian—for any common man to read.

CARLO. We will have to trace the sale of every book, confiscate and destroy it.

POPE. By all means.

CARLO. We'll have to reach out to Galileo.

POPE. He'll hear from us soon enough. But the immediate thing is the book . . . Ciampoli and Riccardi! Bring them here. Bring them here at once.

CARLO. They're on their way. I've ordered them here.

POPE. (*To Major Domo.*) Send a messenger to Ambassador Niccolini. Urgent. Tell him to appear as soon as possible. (*The Major Domo goes. The Pope paces back and forth. He picks up the book and reads a line or two, then marches up and down once more.*)

FRANCESCO. (*Planting himself squarely in front of Pope.*) Uncle, do not do this thing to Galileo's book.

POPE. What!

FRANCESCO. You will betray the millions who look to the Church for guidance and salvation. If you refuse Galileo's ideas you will turn the Church into an inflexible institution, unable to grow as man grows, unable to embrace new truths as man develops them.

POPE. We forbid the existence of a truth unless it be approved by us.

FRANCESCO. You cannot forbid! Truth, like an underground stream, can be stopped up, but some day will rise to the surface. Where will man turn with his new ideas? He will knock at the hard shell of our rigid dogmas and take his new truth elsewhere. And in self-protection we will find ourselves at war against the truth. (*Father Riccardi, Chief Censor of the Press, and Monsignor Ciampoli, Papal Secretary of State, enter.*)

POPE. Do you know this book?

RICCARDI. (*Opens it.*) Why, it's Galileo's.

CIAMPOLI. Look at the engraving of his portrait.

RICCARDI. A becoming likeness.

POPE. (*Icily.*) We will save the esthetic considerations. Did you, as Chief Censor of the Press, allow this book to pass?

RICCARDI. Yes.

POPE. How, as Chief Censor of the Press, did you allow this book to pass?

RICCARDI. He complied with our every instruction. He added a preface outlined by us, and we've changed innumerable sentences in the body of the book. We were very careful. And after we finished, why, naturally, we gave him a license.

CARLO. He complied with all your instructions!

RICCARDI. Oh, yes.

CARLO. And with each compliance, he has increased the difficulties of the Church.

RICCARDI. Your Holiness, what does he mean?

POPE. He means that Galileo's book is detrimental to the faith. He means that this book will damage the authority of the Church. He means that because of this book, religion is imperilled.

RICCARDI. What!

POPE. This book does not deal with mathematics. It deals with faith and reason.

RICCARDI. I have read it through at least a dozen times. I still don't understand.

POPE. You may go! (*Riccardi starts off.*) As for you, Ciampoli, I'll send you to some miserable province where you can spend the rest of your days thinking this over. Wait, Riccardi. (*Riccardi comes forward.*) As your last official act, send an order to the Inquisitor at Florence to confiscate every remaining copy at Landini's bookshop. (*Riccardi is stunned. He and Ciampoli go.*)

FRANCESCO. Uncle, our Church should be a warm mansion for humanity, not a cold prison for his spirit!

POPE. We cannot turn back!

FRANCESCO. Woe unto Christ's Church! We are shutting men away from God. (*He goes.*)

CARLO. I am sorry my son is such a trial to you. When will he grow up and be sensible? (*He goes. Father Firenzuola, who has remained unobtrusively in the shadows, comes forward.*)

POPE. Are you still here, Father Firenzuola?

FIRENZUOLA. Your Holiness, if I judge the signs correctly, the trial of an important man will come before the Inquisition. I have the deepest esteem for the present Commissary General of the Inquisition and believe him perfectly suited for his work in all respects but one—and this one thing, Your Holiness, will prove of paramount importance.

POPE. What is this one thing?

FIRENZUOLA. Pressure. The art of pressure.

POPE. Go on.

FIRENZUOLA. This man who will probably stand trial before the Inquisition claims to love nature and constantly gives examples from it. May I do likewise? (*The Pope nods.*) A frog is dropped into a pot of boiling water. He squirms, he struggles, sometimes leaps out and escapes, and always splashes the spectators and creates a violent stir. Another frog is slipped into a pot of cool water. He is content. He squats comfortably. The water is slowly heated. Gradually, gradually, the heat is increased. The water even boils but the frog does not stir—his senses have become slowly numb. He dies peacefully. The same objective has been accomplished, one by a bungler, the other by an artist. *I am an artist!*

(*During his speech he has gradually moved closer to the Pope. Now he withdraws.*) May I speak further?

POPE. Proceed.

FIRENZUOLA. Your Holiness, the understanding of pressure—how to apply it—when—to what degree—these are the fine techniques of a craft attained only by deep study of the inner workings of a man's heart and brain. To understand the mixture of fear and courage, hope and despair—to make a man's mind war with the fear which is mixed with the marrow of his bones. This subject, Your Holiness, has been my constant study.

POPE. And how do you propose to put your knowledge to use?

FIRENZUOLA. Your Holiness, I have taken the liberty to do some investigating of my own.

POPE. Have you? I hope you have been discreet?

FIRENZUOLA. I am a man of discretion, Your Holiness. It was a matter of only a few moments. There was a file I wanted to look at. In this file, I found some papers. (*He extracts some papers from the sleeve of his robe.*) I think Your Holiness will be interested in reading this document.

POPE. (*Looks at it quickly.*) Where is this from?

FIRENZUOLA. The official file on Galileo Galilei.

MAJOR DOMO. (*Enters.*) Ambassador Niccolini has arrived.

POPE. Bring him in at once, and then get Ciampoli and Riccardi. Be quick. (*The Major Domo hurries out. In absolute silence the Pope stares at Firenzuola in keen appraisal. Firenzuola meets the Pope's gaze on equal terms. Then the Major Domo re-enters, ushering Sagredo in. Sagredo kneels and rises.*)

SAGREDO. I came at once, Your Holiness.

POPE. I swear you to silence as to what you are about to hear and see.

SAGREDO. I swear.

POPE. If you break your oath you place your Catholic soul in jeopardy of eternal damnation. (*To Firenzuola, who has moved a respectful distance aside, a hint of triumph in his bearing.*) Come closer, my good Firenzuola. (*To Sagredo.*) Father Firenzuola performs delicate tasks for me, and is soon due for an important post.

FIRENZUOLA. Thank you, Your Holiness.

POPE. (*To Firenzuola.*) And Messer Niccolini is the Florentine Ambassador to Rome.

FIRENZUOLA. I have known Ambassador Niccolini by fame, I am glad to know him by face.

RICCARDI. (*Enters.*) Yes, Your Holiness?

POPE. Stand there and be quiet.

RICCARDI. Yes, Your Holiness. (*The Pope studies the memorandum. Silence for a moment.*)

CIAMPOLI. (*Enters.*) You sent for me, Your Holi—? (*He is silenced by a gesture from the Pope.*)

POPE. (*Motions Riccardi and Ciampoli to stand together. Then, abruptly.*) When Galileo presented his *Dialogue* and applied for a license, what did he say regarding Cardinal Bellarmin's admonition to him?

RICCARDI. What did he say?

POPE. What were the exact terms of Cardinal Bellarmin's admonition to him? What did he say they were?

RICCARDI. He told me what is common knowledge—our official Catholic stand.

POPE. (*Icily.*) Do not tell us what our official Catholic stand is! Tell us exactly what he told you!

RICCARDI. He said that Cardinal Bellarmin told him that since the system of Copernicus does not agree with Church Doctrine, it therefore cannot be held as a truth, but may be discussed in terms of hypothesis.

POPE. He did not at any time say that Cardinal Bellarmin enjoined *entire* silence upon him, and that he could not hold, teach or defend his doctrine in any way whatsoever!

RICCARDI. Not *even* as hypothesis?

POPE. That he is forbidden to speak about it or write about it *in any way whatsoever*—did he ever tell you this?

CIAMPOLI. No, he did not.

RICCARDI. If there were such an injunction his book would never have passed my hands.

CIAMPOLI. Of course not.

POPE. He would be guilty of writing a book where every word, every letter, every syllable is a sin. Is this not so?

RICCARDI. Yes, Your Holiness.

POPE. He would be guilty of using my patronage to impose on you. Is this not so?

RICCARDI. Yes, Your Holiness. (*Hesitantly.*) Your Holiness, is there such an injunction?

POPE. You have done enough damage! You may go!

RICCARDI. Yes, Your Holiness. (*Ciampoli and Riccardi leave hastily.*)

SAGREDO. *Is* there such an injunction? (*The Pope gives the paper to Sagredo. Though still disturbed, Sagredo is greatly relieved.*) This is obviously not an official document. This is some memorandum written by an overzealous clerk.

POPE. It is part of the permanent records of our Holy Office, taken from our files on Galileo.

SAGREDO. Why, this paper doesn't even have a signature. Not of Cardinal Bellarmin, or any of the witnesses, or of Galileo.

POPE. Do not speak lightly of memoranda from our official files.

SAGREDO. This was not the intention of Pope Gregory XV or of Cardinal Bellarmin when they admonished Galileo.

POPE. Would you like to call them in and ask them their intention?

SAGREDO. Your Holiness knows as well as I that they are both dead.

POPE. Then we'll have to go by our files. This document is—

SAGREDO. Forgive me, Your Holiness, it is not a document. It is an unsigned paper. When was this written —and by whom? Why, it doesn't even have a date. (*He returns it to the Pope.*)

POPE. (*Continuing.*) This document is enough to hand the entire matter over to the Inquisition. It will be for them to determine if Galileo is guilty of concealing the prohibition and of wilfully transgressing it. And remember, Ambassador Niccolini, you have been sworn to secrecy. You know what charges the Inquisition will prefer, but Galileo must not know them until he stands before the judges.

SAGREDO. Galileo will ask my advice both as his friend and his Ambassador. Because of this secret you have thrust upon me I will be of no use to him. Your Holiness, you have tied my hands very effectively.

POPE. Have I?

SAGREDO. But, Your Holiness, there is one thing which perhaps you have overlooked.

POPE. Have I?

SAGREDO. What if, in spite of my oath, I choose to tell Galileo? Only he and I would know of it.

POPE. You would impair your eternal soul.

SAGREDO. I might choose to risk it—my soul for the living truth.

POPE. There is another soul involved. Galileo's! He will know that you have given your oath to me and he will refuse to listen. His Catholic soul is of too great consequence to him.

SAGREDO. (*Bitterly.*) Your Holiness, you have overlooked nothing.

POPE. (*To Firenzuola, who has been discreetly in the*

69

background.) Firenzuola, you will make out the necessary papers as follows: Write to Florence and have Galileo summoned to appear before the Commissary General of the Inquisition in Rome within one month's time.

SAGREDO. (*Shocked.*) Rome! The man is sixty-nine years old. His health is failing and he is nearly blind. Surely he can be tried by the Inquisitors in Florence?

POPE. He must be tried in person and in Rome. (*He gives Firenzuola the memorandum.*)

FIRENZUOLA. The papers will go to Florence at once. (*He goes.*)

SAGREDO. Your Holiness runs the danger of his being tried neither in Florence nor in Rome. For I solemnly assure you he may die on the way.

POPE. If he is not well, he can come slowly—but he will come. In chains, if necessary—but he will come. He must be tried in Rome.

(*The lights dim down sharply, coming up meanwhile on the Convent of St. Matthew of Arcetri. In the darkness, Sagredo and the Pope move off.*)

ACT II

Scene 5

(*The Convent. Galileo and Maria Celeste are present. There is almost no pause between the Pope's last speech and Maria Celeste's first speech.*)

MARIA CELESTE. But you can't go to Rome at this time of the year. The winds coming down from the mountains are too cold. Wait until spring.

GALILEO. I cannot wait. I have not been *invited* to Rome. I have been ordered to Rome. I must go.

MARIA CELESTE. No, Father! . . . But why? You have obeyed every injunction. (*Raises her right hand.*) I who have copied out the book with this hand am witness to it.

GALILEO. I must go to Rome. There I'll find out. . . . It seems we have not yet earned our right to sit here in peace and quiet. And I have little time left.

MARIA CELESTE. We are but strangers and pilgrims. Dear pilgrim, be comforted.

GALILEO. Good-bye, Sister Maria Celeste.

MARIA CELESTE. I shall pray for you every day. (*The lights dim down sharply, coming up meanwhile on the terrace of Sagredo's palace. Galileo moves into the scene, as Sagredo moves into it from the other side. There is no pause between Maria Celeste's last speech and Sagredo's first speech.*)

ACT II

Scene 6

The terrace of Sagredo's palace. It is night time and there is a bright moon.

SAGREDO. You must keep this one thought fixed firmly in your mind. You must do everything possible to shorten the proceedings. Be acquiescent. Be humble. Be submissive. When they say Yes, you say Yes. When they say No, you say No.

GALILEO. But if I cannot say Yes to their Yes, or No to their No?

SAGREDO. Then say—"Perhaps it is so," or "I do not remember."

GALILEO. "Perhaps it is so." "I do not remember."

SAGREDO. Do not cross them—pacify them. Do not defend your work—if you do they will be all the more certain to condemn it. Remember, be acquiescent—be submissive. Be humble.

GALILEO. "Perhaps it is so." "I do not remember."

SAGREDO. You must do whatever necessary to shorten the proceedings.

GALILEO. Be acquiescent. Be humble. Yes, Yes—No, No. "Perhaps it is so." "I do not remember." (*With a cry of anguish.*) Have I outlived my years? If I had died the day the first book came off the press! My life going into the life of the book. Wouldn't that have been better? Oh, Sagredo, I am so tired.

SAGREDO. We'll get you out of Rome and back to

72

Florence where you still have years of work ahead of you.

GALILEO. Do you think they know that I've already come?

SAGREDO. They knew within the hour. For all I know, some of my own servants inform for the Inquisition—my servants who helped you out of the litter, my Major Domo. No one knows who is an informer—yet everyone may be. Yes, they know you have come.

GALILEO. If I but knew the charges I could think along those lines. I could try to—

SAGREDO. I know the charges against you.

GALILEO. You do!

SAGREDO. It is one single charge. They will accuse you of—

GALILEO. Sagredo, how did you find out?

SAGREDO. His Holiness told me.

GALILEO. And then swore you to secrecy?

SAGREDO. Naturally.

GALILEO. You have given your oath before God. I will not listen.

SAGREDO. I was afraid of this.

GALILEO. (*Looks out over terrace.*) There's the Vatican, where His Holiness may be sleeping at this very moment. We were so near to each other. If I could see him face to face—but he will not see me. Look! The Flower Market! Where they burn heretics! What is it like when the smoke thickens, when the flame creeps up, when body and soul separate? (*With a cry of terror.*) Sagredo—! (*He leaves the thought unstated.*)

SAGREDO. It is getting cold. Let us go inside.

GALILEO. (*Shakes his head in the negative, indicating that he wishes to be alone. Sagredo goes. Galileo is alone and distraught. Suddenly, the Major Domo enters; a black cape partially conceals his uniform. Galileo is terrified.*)

73

Scene setting ? Transition

ACT II, SCENE 6

MAJOR DOMO. I am not here to harm you. (*The Major Domo signals and Two Guards, with drawn swords, enter. Their uniforms, too, are partially concealed by black capes.*) They are deaf and dumb. I, who can hear and speak, must go. (*He signals again and goes. The Pope enters.*)

GALILEO. Your Holiness!

POPE. Galileo, you have placed my soul in jeopardy. I am in danger of eternal damnation!

GALILEO. Your Holiness!

POPE. From the days of Constantine, thirteen hundred years ago, when Catholic Christianity emerged triumphant, the Church has had to war with heresy, building always the foundation of a new Europe, a Catholic Europe. We have had to fight Luther in Germany, Calvin and Zwingli in Switzerland, Huss in Bohemia, Wycliffe in England, the Huguenots in France, the Anabaptists, the Unitarians, the Trinitarians, and a whole host of other heretical Protestant movements—each encouraging intellectual anarchy, with every man thinking differently from his neighbor. In recent times the printing press and the indiscriminate dissemination of learning; Columbus and Magellan and the spreading out of the curved earth, have all challenged us. The battle is becoming too severe, too critical—the odds are beginning to shift against us. I have manoeuvred for the position of power, not for myself, but to extend the power of the Catholic Church. But now, Galileo, because of you, I may fail. Your telescope is a burning glass setting Europe on fire. Your book shakes the structure of Christian society. . . . People are saying that if the earth is only one among several planets, it cannot be that any great salvation has been planned for it, that perhaps God has begotten not one, but many sons, sending one to each of your planets! . . . And if I do not win, what

74

can I do, what can I say, how can I plead when I come face to face with my Creator and have to account for my life? My soul will be judged with Lucifer's and I will face eternal damnation.

GALILEO. So it comes to this: The salvation of your soul depends upon the temporal success of the Church. And since I am an enemy of the Church, the salvation of your soul depends upon my destruction!

POPE. Oh, Galileo! Say no more! My soul is in anguish; my nights are a torment. I live in dread that your words will soar straight up to the throne of God.

GALILEO. You can order men what to believe, but not what to see; the conclusions of science are matters not of opinion, but of demonstration. The day will yet come when the scientific understanding of Nature will be the highest demonstration of the glory of God. Time, which is on the side of science, will be my judge —and will bring about that day, that light, in which God's work and mine will be revealed as one. . . . But for now, today, this minute—what is my comfort? Listen. Looking all through my works, no one can find the least shadow which deviates from love and veneration for Holy Mother Church. I say now that my Catholic soul is whole before God! The Mystery of the Mass is true and dear to me. It is of my deepest faith. Till my dying day I will cry out the glory of God! . . . I have no more to say except this: Your Holiness, before you go, since you are Christ's Vicar on earth, I beg of you, bless me. (*The Pope hesitates.*) You cannot refuse!

POPE. (*Gestures the benediction, then kneels beside the kneeling Galileo. Tenderly, he takes Galileo's face in his hands. He speaks with infinite sorrow and regret.*) Farewell, Galileo! We will not see each other again. (*He rises, signals the Two Guards, and, flanking him, the three move off quickly.*)

Act II, Scene 6

GALILEO. (*Is still on his knees. He lifts his hands in prayer.*) Oh, Lord, hear my prayer! And it is not for myself. It is for the salvation of the soul of Maffeo Barberini!

BLACKOUT

END OF ACT II

ACT III

Scene 1

The Inquisitorial Chambers. The year is 1633.
The room is empty and in bright sunshine. A Clerk
enters with quills, ink and papers, seats himself and
prepares his records. A Dominican Monk enters.
He arranges the table and three chairs. He places
a Bible and a crucifix on the table. Then the three
Inquisitors enter. Father Firenzuola, now Commis-
sary General of the Holy Office, seats himself in
center chair; the other two seat themselves at either
end. Silently Firenzuola passes various papers to
them.

FIRENZUOLA. (*To the Dominican.*) Call the attend-
ant. (*The Dominican goes to door and beckons. The*
Attendant, also a Dominican, quickly enters. Then, to
Attendant.) He is outside?
ATTENDANT. He has been waiting for a long time.
FIRENZUOLA. Waiting induces penitence.
ATTENDANT. Yes, Father. (*The First Dominican*
draws various shade cords, throwing the room in deep
gloom. He pulls one cord; a single shaft of blinding sun-
light floods in.) Shall I bring him in now?
FIRENZUOLA. The hearing is scheduled for nine. We
will wait until the bells ring.
ATTENDANT. Yes, Father. (*There is absolutely no*
movement as they all wait. Then church bells ring.)
FIRENZUOLA. (*On the ninth stroke.*) Let him come
in.

77

ATTENDANT. Yes, Father. (*He goes, comes back immediately, leading Galileo, whom he places in the shaft of light. The two Dominicans leave immediately. The three Inquisitors continue studying their briefs. Galileo stands, straining his sight against the light. The Inquisitors put down their briefs.*)

FIRENZUOLA. In the name of the Father, the Son and the Holy Ghost, I open these proceedings. (*Everyone makes the sign of the cross. Firenzuola to the Inquisitor nearest Galileo, indicating Bible.*) Give it to him. (*The Inquisitor does. Firenzuola to Galileo.*) Repeat after me.

FIRENZUOLA and GALILEO. I solemnly swear to answer with the truth all questions asked of me, withholding nothing; and to abide with Christian resignation by the inspired decision of my reverend judges. This I swear holding in my hand the Holy Bible and bearing in my heart the dread of the Lord before whose judgment stands my naked soul.

FIRENZUOLA. (*As the Clerk begins to write.*) Your name?

GALILEO. Galileo Galilei.

FIRENZUOLA. Your age?

GALILEO. Seventy years.

FIRENZUOLA. Your occupation?

GALILEO. Scientist.

FIRENZUOLA. Pay attention to what I say. I must remind the accused that he has it in his power to shorten these proceedings.

GALILEO. How is it in my power?

FIRENZUOLA. It is our experience that of the accused brought before these hearings there are those who quickly confess and throw themselves on our mercy; and there are those who do not confess, who when examined and questioned at length with all the facilities and ingenuity of this Holy Office—

78

GALILEO. You mean torture!

FIRENZUOLA. —are found guilty and convicted of heresy. For these heretics the Church has but short patience! Therefore, before we proceed, is there anything you wish to tell this court? Is there something burdening your conscience? (*Galileo is frightened, but silent.*) Then there is nothing you wish to tell this court, nothing burdens your conscience? (*Another silence.*) We will proceed. You have been ordered to appear before the Inquisition of the Holy Office. Do you know why?

GALILEO. I have not been told officially, but I believe that it is because of my book.

FIRENZUOLA. Go on.

GALILEO. My book called *A Dialogue on Two Systems of the World.*

FIRENZUOLA. (*Produces the book.*) Will the accused look at this book? (*Galileo takes it.*) Do you recognize it?

GALILEO. It's a copy of my book, *The Dialogue.*

FIRENZUOLA. And you are fully responsible for every thought expressed, every word written in it?

GALILEO. I am.

FIRENZUOLA. We will now go back to the year of our Lord 1616. Where were you then?

GALILEO. Do you mean was I in Rome?

FIRENZUOLA. Were you?

GALILEO. I was.

FIRENZUOLA. Why were you summoned to Rome?

GALILEO. Summoned? I was not summoned! I came of my own free will. (*The Inquisitors eye him silently.*) I was not ordered to come! (*Silence.*) I had nothing to do with the Inquisition!

FIRENZUOLA. Oh!

GALILEO. (*Rushes on.*) I was not personally involved. I came as a scientist to acquaint the Church with a new

79

truth, and as a Catholic to be told what to believe. (*Silence.*) Look in your records—there's no summons there for me.

FIRENZUOLA. In the year of our Lord 1616, a decision was handed down to you by the Holy Congregation of the Index. Exactly what was the decision?

GALILEO. Cardinal Bellarmin told me it was contrary to Church Doctrine to say that the earth moves and that the sun does not move. However, although this opinion could not be held as an established fact, it could be held as a supposition—a mathematical hypothesis.

FIRENZUOLA. The Court has not interrupted you.

GALILEO. But I've just told you the decision. He said that it could not be stated in its *absolute* sense, but that it could be held as a hypothetical proposition—a theory.

FIRENZUOLA. Tell the Court how you were informed of this decision.

GALILEO. Cardinal Bellarmin told it to me.

FIRENZUOLA. Cardinal Bellarmin has been dead for years.

GALILEO. His death does not change the status of this case.

FIRENZUOLA. (*He is utterly surprised.*) What did you say?

GALILEO. I said, his death does not change the status of this case. To protect me then and for the future, Cardinal Bellarmin gave me a written memorandum of our conversation. I have brought it here and want to introduce it into the records. (*He hands it to Firenzuola, who looks at it, then passes it to others.*)

FIRENZUOLA. (*With sharpness.*) Come forward! (*The Inquisitor to the left hands Firenzuola some records.*) Here is *our* record of the interview. (*Reads.*) "—Galileo, having been summoned and appearing, Cardinal Bellarmin warned Galileo of his opinions and or-

80

dered him to abandon them. Then the Chief Inquisitor Michael Angelo Segnezzio *commanded* Galileo in the name of His Holiness the Pope to relinquish *altogether* the doctrine—" (*His voice sinks, during which time Galileo utters an urgent "No, No," then rises emphatically.*) "—nor henceforth to hold, teach or defend in any way whatsoever, verbally or in writing, otherwise proceedings would be taken against him."

GALILEO. No! No! Only Cardinal Bellarmin spoke to me.

FIRENZUOLA. Do you say that our records are incorrect?

GALILEO. (*Pointing to his memorandum.*) This is Cardinal Bellarmin's handwriting. You can see for yourself.

FIRENZUOLA. (*Holding one up in each hand.*) Here are two sets of records. Whose are to be relied upon? Yours or ours? (*Galileo is staggered.*) We will proceed. So, after Cardinal Bellarmin's warning, you were then commanded and enjoined by Chief Inquisitor Segnezzio not to teach the Copernican doctrine in any way whatsoever—even as hypothesis.

GALILEO. It may be so.

FIRENZUOLA. Were you or weren't you?

GALILEO. It may be so, but I do not remember.

FIRENZUOLA. You do not remember?

GALILEO. It was seventeen years ago and I took no pains to impress the exact words in my mind. After all, I had Cardinal Bellarmin's memorandum.

FIRENZUOLA. So you received a command—

GALILEO. It may be so, but I do not remember. I remember only Cardinal Bellarmin's talk with me.

FIRENZUOLA. Disobeying this command, you set about writing this book. Tell me, did you ask for permission to write this book?

81

GALILEO. No.

FIRENZUOLA. Why not?

GALILEO. Because I did not think I had disobeyed any command.

FIRENZUOLA. So you wrote the book without permission. And when you applied for the license to print the book, did you tell our official censors about the injunction against you?

GALILEO. No.

FIRENZUOLA. Why not?

GALILEO. Because I did not think I had disobeyed any command.

FIRENZUOLA. One more question. In a dialogue, the author introduces two characters who advance opposing sets of arguments—each attempting, by the force of his logic, to win the other over. Is that correct?

GALILEO. The author presents every argument, no matter to which side it belongs. He reasons for and against with equal force, but does not take a position himself.

FIRENZUOLA. (*With anger.*) Do not try to throw sand in our eyes! Credit us with as much skill and understanding as you have. This so-called impartiality is the artifice by which the author drives home his points, yet evades the responsibility for his opinions. Let us proceed.

GALILEO. Yes, Father.

FIRENZUOLA. In your book you pit a Copernican against an Aristotelian. In whose mouth did you put the more forceful arguments?

GALILEO. What are you making me do?

FIRENZUOLA. We make you do nothing. We must ascertain the facts.

GALILEO. (*Shouting.*) I curse my years of study! I

would suppress and burn every word that I've ever
written if I could!

FIRENZUOLA. (*Very quietly.*) You had better answer. We must know your intentions—whether your
bias was deliberate or accidental. I repeat the question:
To which system did you give the stronger arguments?
To Aristotle and the movement of the sun, or to Copernicus and the movement of the earth?

GALILEO. I am here in your hands—do with me as
you please.

FIRENZUOLA. You are here to answer this question!
(*Galileo is silent.*) I put the question to you for the last
time. In your book did you or did you not favor the
opinion that the earth is not the center of the universe?

GALILEO. (*Slowly.*) Before the decision of the
Church I regarded both opinions open to discussion.
But once the Church in her inspired wisdom decreed
that the earth is stationary and that the sun moves
around it, I knew that I must so believe.

FIRENZUOLA. Then why did you write the book?

GALILEO. I'm in your hands—do with me what you
please.

FIRENZUOLA. You are here to obey! Answer.

GALILEO. My purpose was to present both sides of
the case, and show the reader that neither set of arguments is conclusive, and the only way to be certain of
the truth is to fall back on the higher teachings of the
Church. I am in your hands—do with me what you
please.

FIRENZUOLA. (*To Clerk.*) Are you finished? (*The
Clerk nods affirmatively.*)

FIRENZUOLA. Bring it here. (*The Clerk does.*) I
call the examination to a close. (*To Galileo.*) Accused,
you will sign the minutes of this hearing. (*Galileo,
without looking at them, does. Meanwhile Firenzuola*

signals the Clerk, who goes to the door and signals.)
Repeat after me this oath.

FIRENZUOLA and GALILEO. With my hands on
this Bible, I solemnly swear that my lips will be sealed
with the seal of silence. Neither by word nor sign will
I betray what has passed here. (*Two Dominicans enter
as the oath is finished, take Galileo by the arm and lead
him off. In dim light they are seen to lead him to his
room in the Palace of the Inquisition on the other side
of the stage.*)

FIRST INQUISITOR. (*To Firenzuola.*) Well, Father,
what do you think?

FIRENZUOLA. He has already damaged himself badly. We can imprison him if necessary. But I must confess that I am bitterly disappointed.

FIRST INQUISITOR. Why, Father Firenzuola?

FIRENZUOLA. Because he denies absolutely that he
has overstepped the injunction. He insists he was within his rights.

FIRST INQUISITOR. And he does have Cardinal
Bellarmin's memorandum to support his claim.

FIRENZUOLA. We will accomplish little without a
confession. The misguided may even place a halo
around his head—a martyr to science. But if he confesses
freely, this trial will be a great success. We will show
Galileo weak, insincere, of no integrity. We will wreck
his influence. One more danger to the Church will be
eliminated. I must have his free confession! I will be
satisfied with nothing less. (*With sudden realization.*)
I have the key. I know how to unlock this man. I will
get his confession. Believe me—I will get his confession!
(*Firenzuola begins walking toward Galileo's room.
Light dims down on the scene of the Inquisitorial
Chamber, and then, as Firenzuola moves out of it, light
blacks out entirely. Meanwhile, lights come up on Gal-*

*ileo's room in the Palace of the Inquisition. Firenzuola
moves into the scene. There is no pause in time between
Firenzuola's last word "confession," and his first speech
in next scene.)*

ACT III

Scene 2

Galileo's room in the Palace of the Inquisition.

FIRENZUOLA. (*Trying to force a paper on Galileo. Galileo holds back.*) There are questions of far greater importance than those propounded in mathematics. There are questions relating to ethics, to our relation to God, to our future. It is irrelevant to me whether Jupiter has four planets or none—there is something more important than that. If our soul is to perish, whether in eighty or eighty million years, this period of time is only an executioner's grace. Besides our material world there is a spiritual world, infinitely richer than the one in which we live, a world of which we are to become a part. (*Thrusting forth the paper.*) Take it!

GALILEO. No! No! I have no confession to make! I will answer the questions and if you find me guilty you can punish me. But I have no confession to make.

FIRENZUOLA. Read it!

GALILEO. It is my confession. I will not read it.

FIRENZUOLA. The world trembles on the edge of ruin. Only the unity of Christendom can hold mankind together. But this unity stands on a series of beliefs about the relationship of God, man and the world. The man who threatens this unity threatens the world.

GALILEO. (*Pushing the paper away.*) No!

FIRENZUOLA. You are that man, Galileo. You are destroying the unity of the world. You have become a man of chaos.

GALILEO. No. No. I will not give you a confession.

FIRENZUOLA. You say you are innocent. By what standard? Your own mind! And if it is wrong? And if the Prince of Darkness has fastened himself upon you and at this very moment you are his servant, performing his work? Is there no doubt at all in your mind? Somewhere, deep, deep, there *is* the shadow of doubt. Think, Galileo, think! The unity of the Church rests in your hands. If there is the shadow of a shadow of doubt in your mind, and you smother that doubt, then all the villains of the world, Luther, Calvin, and the rest, will be as saints compared to you. They left the Church and attacked her from without! But you, you will destroy what you claim to love. Think! Dare you assume this awful responsibility? What of your soul? Forever the fires of hell will rage and consume your soul, and consume it, and consume it, and yet never consume it—eternally there for the fire.

GALILEO. (*Has taken the paper, looks at it.*) Horrible! Horrible! "Vainglorious ambition!—Vulgar complacence!—Vanity!" Is this what I am to say about myself? (*Throws it to the floor.*)

FIRENZUOLA. (*Picks it up and forces it into Galileo's hands.*) Do not draw back—for your soul's sake. Do not draw back. Taking this paper out of my hand is a step forward, a barrier destroyed, the beginning of our victory. You object to a few words—perhaps too severe. And would you let a few words stand in your way? Galileo, man is a spiritual being with a supernatural destiny; his destiny is the only thing that matters supremely. Do not let it slip away from you! I will plead with you and I will pray with you until you realize the indwelling presence of God through the surrender of your will to Him. Come, pray. (*Galileo is shaken, stares*

87

at the paper. Firenzuola begins.) "When my hands, cold and trembling—"

GALILEO. The Prayer for the Dead!

FIRENZUOLA. (*Softly.*) Pray with me.

FIRENZUOLA and GALILEO. (*Firenzuola's voice is strong and resolute, while Galileo's voice is low and faltering. Gradually Galileo's voice rises in intensity as Firenzuola's diminishes. By the end of the scene, Firenzuola's voice is barely heard, while Galileo's dominates the prayer.*) "When my hands, cold and trembling, shall no longer be able to clasp the crucifix, and against my will shall let it fall on my bed of suffering, merciful God, have mercy on me. When my imagination, agitated by dreadful spectres, shall be sunk in an abyss of anguish; when my soul, affrighted with the sight of my iniquities and the terror of Thy judgments, shall have to fight against the angel of darkness, who will endeavor to conceal Thy mercy from mine eyes, merciful Jesus, have mercy on me. When mine ears, soon to be forever closed to the discourse of men, shall be open to hear the irrevocable decree which is to fix my doom for all eternity, merciful Jesus, have mercy on me." (*Lights have been fading slowly. Now there is a*)

BLACKOUT

88

ACT III

Scene 3

(*Lights come up immediately on a meeting of Cardinals in the Palace of the Inquisition. It is toward the end of a long and difficult session. Everyone is weary; nerves are frayed. The tribunal is composed of Pope Urban VIII, presiding over Father Firenzuola, and these ten: Cardinal Borgia, Cardinal De Ascoli, Cardinal Bentivoglio, Cardinal De Cremona, Cardinal Antonio Barberini, Cardinal Zacchia, Cardinal Gessi, Cardinal Verospi, Cardinal Francesco Barberini and Cardinal Ginetti. Carlo Barberini is there, though not a member of the tribunal. . . . It is to be noted that the only new character with a speaking role in this scene is Cardinal Borgia.*)

FIRENZUOLA. (*Reading.*) "I, the said Galileo Galilei, have abjured, sworn, promised, and bound myself as above; and in witness of the truth thereof, I have with my own hand subscribed the present document of my abjuration, and recited it word for word at Rome, this 22nd day of June 1633. . . . I, Galileo Galilei, have abjured as above with my own hand." Then, Your Eminences, after Galileo reads his recantation, he will rise from his knees and the two Dominicans will lead him from the Church into the room assigned to him.

POPE. Your Eminences, Father Firenzuola has just read Galileo's sentence and the abjuration which he will make. The procedure has been carefully outlined, and

89

if there is no further discussion, all that remains before we adjourn is for you to sign the sentence. Firenzuola, pass the quills to their Eminences. (*Firenzuola passes several quills around.*)

BORGIA. Firenzuola, would you reread one part of this sentence?

FIRENZUOLA. If Your Eminence wishes it.

BORGIA. Toward the end—something about a grave and pernicious error.

FIRENZUOLA. (*Reading.*) "And in order that this your grave and pernicious error—"?

BORGIA. Yes, that's it.

FIRENZUOLA. "And in order that this your grave and pernicious error may not remain altogether unpunished, and as an example to others, that they may abstain from similar delinquencies, we ordain that the book *The Dialogue of Galileo Galilei* be prohibited and publicly burnt."

BORGIA. I object to the burning of the book. It is enough to prohibit it.

FIRENZUOLA. It is *not* enough! We must make a public demonstration to impress on the people the sanctity of our authority. Burn it!

POPE. I incline to Borgia's view. The burning would be too dramatic. Let us be moderate. Firenzuola, change it from "public burning" to "public prohibition."

FIRENZUOLA. I will do so, Your Holiness. But there are times when we must not relax our stern duty.

BORGIA. If Firenzuola had his way he would burn every book and every Christian in Christendom. Who would remain? We thirteen in this room?

FIRENZUOLA. And perhaps some of us would not be above violent suspicion of heresy.

BORGIA. You dare! (*Cardinals break out into the following: "Borgia is right," "Borgia, be quiet," "This should not be allowed," "Borgia, be careful," "He's*

right," "What is he doing," "I agree," "Borgia, Borgia,"
"Borgia is at it again.")
POPE. Enough! Enough! (*There is absolute silence.*)
Let the document be signed. Firenzuola, will you pass
it to Cardinal De Cremona? (*De Cremona signs.*) And
now to Cardinal Verospi. (*Verospi signs.*) Cardinal
Borgia.
BORGIA. (*Quill in hand.*) Your Holiness, you ask us
to sign. After we have signed, will this document re-
ceive your official ratification?
POPE. Borgia, you have been a stumbling block dur-
ing these entire proceedings. You know I cannot sign
this document.
BORGIA. It will have our signature but not yours.
Thus Galileo will be condemned and punished by this
Tribunal of Cardinals—but not by the Pope. Will Your
Holiness deign to advise us why you will not sign,
though you ask us to do it?
POPE. Borgia, you are asking me to go over ground
with which we are all familiar.
BORGIA. Some of us may not be as deeply versed in
these niceties as Your Holiness.
POPE. (*Holding it up.*) You know as well as I that
were I to sign this document I would be placing the future authority of the Catholic Church in grave danger.
BORGIA. Grave danger?
POPE. (*He speaks with deep concern.*) We have de-
clared that the motion of the earth is both false and
contrary to Holy Scripture. Excellent for the present.
But the Church of Rome is not an institution for one
day or one century. Let us imagine that in the future
Galileo should be proven correct. Heretics and infidels
would point the finger and say, "An infallible Pope sitting *ex cathedra* has signed a false document." How
will we guardians of the Church, who must hand over
to our successors an unimpaired institution, how will

91

we have discharged our duties? . . . Yet Galileo must be silenced! The urgent needs of religion demand it! . . . But assume that this tribunal *alone* signs the document and it proves to be in error. The infallibility of the Pope is not involved and Roman Catholic posterity will show that this Tribunal was in error as *men*, but not as an *institution*. Thus, by employing caution and foresight, we avoid the thorns that beset our path, yet pluck the roses!

BORGIA. Leaving us with the thorns! We are lackeys, not cardinals! You have us sit in council only when you wish to cover up your blunders! (*He snaps the quill and throws it on the table. There is a general noisy reaction.*)

POPE. (*There is grief in his voice.*) You are squabbling before Christ's Vicar on earth. Have you no shame? (*Suddenly the room is dead silent. The Pope, very quietly.*) Firenzuola, pass the document around.

FIRENZUOLA. Yes, Your Holiness. (*Firenzuola passes it to Cardinal Gessi, who signs. Then it is passed to Francesco, who drops the quill on the table.*)

POPE. (*Hurt.*) Francesco! Nephew!

FRANCESCO. I speak to you as my Holy Father and as my uncle. I cannot sign this with a clear conscience.

POPE. (*To Carlo.*) Brother, speak to him.

CARLO. Let us recognize our unpleasant duty and get it over with.

FRANCESCO. In this one thing I will follow my conscience. As a member of the Holy Office, I will keep my silence before the outside world—but here, at this meeting, *I will speak!* Posterity will condemn us for our persecution of Galileo as we today condemn the judges of Socrates. (*Snaps his quill, throws it on the table.*) Firenzuola, my congratulations! You have achieved an equivocal immortality. Through the halls of time you will be known as the scoundrel who tricked Galileo into signing his confession.

FIRENZUOLA. I did what was necessary.

FRANCESCO. Scorpion!

FIRENZUOLA. (*With fine irony, to Pope.*) Your Holiness, your nephew is insulting me.

FRANCESCO. (*To Bentivoglio.*) Bentivoglio, you studied under Galileo. Don't sign!

POPE. Bentivoglio! (*Bentivoglio signs. The document is before Zacchia. Silently he drops his quill.*)

FRANCESCO. (*With kindly concern.*) My friend— not you. I'm the nephew of the Pope—Borgia is the Spanish Ambassador. But you, Zacchia—no. The motion will be carried in any case, and Galileo sentenced. Go back and sign.

ZACCHIA. Galileo's work will survive, but we will be as dead men. I have done many things in my life—but not this! (*He snaps the quill and throws it down. He leaves the room, followed by Francesco and Borgia. There is sorrow, even anguish, in the room.*)

POPE. (*Quietly; there is an undertone of grief.*) Let us proceed. Firenzuola, Cardinal De Ascoli is waiting to sign.

FIRENZUOLA. Yes, Your Holiness. (*Firenzuola passes the document to De Ascoli, who is signing it, as . . .*)

BLACKOUT

ACT III

Scene 4

The Church of St. Minerva.
Galileo, clothed as a penitent, pinioned in a shaft
of clear light as from a high window, is on his knees
reading the recantation. Two Dominican Monks
stand quite a bit to the rear of Galileo. The rising
rows are crowded with church dignitaries. Firen-
zuola is present. The Pope is not in the scene.

GALILEO. I, Galileo Galilei, citizen of Florence, seventy years old, kneeling before you, having before my eyes and touching with my hands this Holy Bible, swear that I have always believed, do now believe, and with God's help will forevermore believe, every article which the Holy Catholic and Apostolic Church of Rome holds true and preaches. And now since I am suspected of heresy, having falsely held that the sun is the center of the universe, and also that the earth is not the center, and that it moves, I am anxious to remove from the minds of my judges and from the minds of all faithful Christians this ugly suspicion so reasonably entertained against me. Therefore with a sincere heart I now abjure, detest and curse these errors and heresies. I swear that in the future I will never say or write anything which may raise similar suspicion against me. Furthermore, I swear that if I know any heretic, or anyone suspected of heresy, I will denounce him to the

94

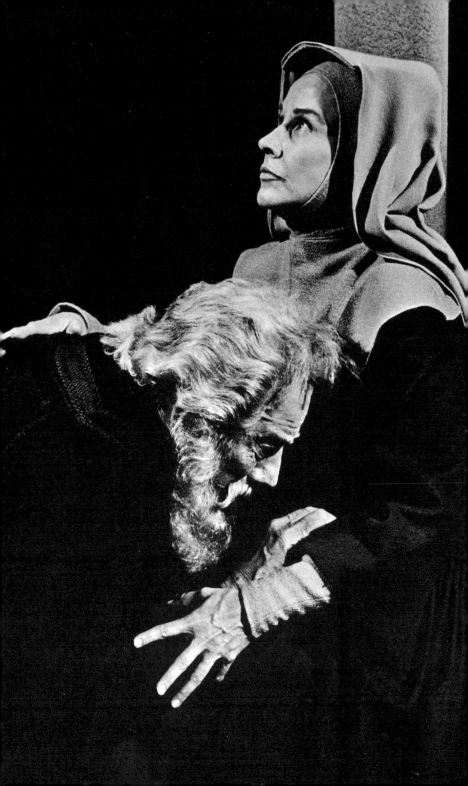

Inquisition. I, Galileo Galilei, have abjured, sworn and promised, and hold myself bound, so help me God. And in witness sign my name in the presence of the Inquisition. (*As he signs.*) Galileo Galilei! (*There is a*)

BLACKOUT

ACT III

Scene 5

The Convent. Maria Celeste and Mother Superior. Maria Celeste is sick and frail. There is a small brazier before Maria Celeste, and she is feeding Galileo's letters to the flames.

MOTHER SUPERIOR. Why can't it wait? Why must you burn them today?

MARIA CELESTE. I must. I feel death coming close. When it comes, and you go through my possessions, there may be something, I don't know what, that will be used against him.

MOTHER SUPERIOR. But I would not send anything that would harm your father!

MARIA CELESTE. It would be your duty. It's better this way. I've saved them. Every note, every word he ever sent me. Now there will not be a scrap left. I've prayed for life long enough to see him, and God has heard my prayers.

MOTHER SUPERIOR. When the spring sun comes you'll be well.

MARIA CELESTE. Mother, my fever burns me. I will not live until spring. I will not see the sun or the stars much longer. Mother, don't weep. Be happy with me for God's goodness. I shall see my father once more. God is infinitely good. (*Maria Celeste has finished the letters. Now she is trying to tear Galileo's book.*)

MOTHER SUPERIOR. What are you doing to his book?

MARIA CELESTE. It has been forbidden by Rome. Mother, help me. I cannot tear it alone. (*Together they crack and dismember the book. Maria Celeste drops a section of the book into fire.*) Books should not be burnt! (*With a cry she reaches into the flames. The Mother Superior pulls her hands back.*) Mother, help me. His Holiness must be right, yet my father cannot be wrong. Mother, help me— (*She is in the arms of the Mother Superior.*)

MOTHER SUPERIOR. My daughter—my daughter! We must not try to understand. Here we are behind these walls. We must only believe, and pray—pray without ceasing for the sins of man and for the pain of the world.

MARIA CELESTE. (*Pulls herself together. Very quietly.*) His note said before sundown. (*She moves toward the steps.*)

MOTHER SUPERIOR. Rest, daughter, I'll go. (*She does.*) There is someone turning the bend in the road.

MARIA CELESTE. Is it my father?

MOTHER SUPERIOR. He's been gone a year, hasn't he?

MARIA CELESTE. Six months in Rome—six months in exile.

MOTHER SUPERIOR. The year has not been kind to him. Be strong.

MARIA CELESTE. Mother, leave us alone and let none of the other sisters come out. (*The Mother Superior goes. Maria Celeste sits on the bench, sings and accompanies herself on the lute.*)

"Oh, darkened house, oh, widowed window,
    say,
Where is that sun that lately from thee shone?
That smiled, and made such brightness on the
    way?
And now—what see I? Tears on every stone!

97

And now I see the very stones in pain,
Oh, window, that may never shine again!"
(*Toward the end of the song Galileo walks in from the
other side, tired and old. He stands for a long moment
at the far end. Her song wavers. She puts her lute down
and opens her arms to him. He goes to her, falling on
his knees, burying his head in her lap.*)
GALILEO. Polissena! Polissena!
MARIA CELESTE. Sssh! . . .
GALILEO. All my life I've needed only two things.
My Bible and my telescope. I have betrayed them both.
I put my hand on the Bible—on the Bible!—and swore
falsely about my science!
MARIA CELESTE. God understands many things and
God reconciles the opposite ends of a man which seem
to contradict each other. In the good eyes of God you
are a religious man and a great scientist. (*She takes a
rose that is lying on the table.*) Today I found a wild
winter rose. I am glad I have it to give you. (*She gives
it to him.*) And with this rose you must accept its
thorns, the symbols of the bitter passion of our Lord.
And let the green leaves be as a hope that we shall pass
through the darkness of winter and come to the bright-
ness of spring—which may our gracious God grant us
through His mercy.
GALILEO. You do not look very well.
MARIA CELESTE. A slight fever.
GALILEO. (*Takes her hands.*) Your hands are cold.
Here. (*Leads her to the brazier.*) Warm them. (*She
does.*) If I picked up a coal and held it clenched in my
fist till the flesh charred, and then when fire met bone,
pressed it over my heart, would the fire eat into my
heart? How long does it take before there is no more
hurt?
MARIA CELESTE. You mustn't talk this way.

98

GALILEO. Why didn't I let them burn me? Why didn't I let them burn me?

MARIA CELESTE. You were right to choose life. Religion may need martyrs, but science needs the living.

GALILEO. My name is forbidden. My writings are on the Index. All my books must be destroyed. Why live?

MARIA CELESTE. You will still *work*.

GALILEO. To what end? I'm forbidden to publish anything I write.

MARIA CELESTE. It *will* be published. Maybe not now, maybe in a different time from ours. What you have done and what you will do may help another scientist many years from now.

GALILEO. (*It is a cry of anguish.*) Sister, support my faith!

MARIA CELESTE. When I used to copy your notes on the mechanics of force and motion, you told me it was an untouched field of science, waiting to be explored. Start work again on experiments of force and equilibrium. . . . Father, I was only a child, but I remember the night you implored Libri and the others to help you spread the truth. You said that there were wastelands to be explored, frontiers of knowledge to be enlarged. Then when your book was published, you came here. You said that ignorance was a curse, and that poverty and disease sprang from it. Why, Father, every scrap of learning, every fact observed and recorded, is an assault on this ignorance, this poverty, this disease. This is true! And being true, you cannot stop your work! Promise me you will work. *Promise me!*

GALILEO. Polissena, your hands are so cold.

MARIA CELESTE. Promise me!

GALILEO. I promise.

MARIA CELESTE. You will make a sword of your sorrow! (*The Angelus rings.*)

GALILEO. I must pray. As part of my sentence I am ordered to recite the Penitential Psalms one day a week. This is the day.

MARIA CELESTE. I know. I have obtained permission to say them for you.

GALILEO. Polissena!

MARIA CELESTE. To do your penance for you gives me joy. Rest, Father. (*Galileo sits on one side as Maria Celeste begins the Penitential Psalms.*) "Have mercy upon me, oh God, according to Thy loving kindness. For I acknowledge my faults, and my sin is ever before me. Oh, Lord, do not despise my broken and contrite heart. Cast me not away from Thy presence, and take not Thy Holy Spirit from me. Oh, give me the comfort of Thy help again. Glory be to the Father and to the Son, and to the Holy Ghost. World without end. Amen." (*She pauses in silent meditation. Galileo, on the other side of the stage, speaks in soliloquy; Maria Celeste does not hear him. Their speeches produce an antiphonal effect.*)

GALILEO. On my knees I was forced to deny my own self and my knowledge of the laws of the universe. You can destroy every telescope, smash every lens, burn every book; you can command the race of man to lower his eyes to the earth like the lowest animal, you can tear out the eyes of every offender who dares lift his head to the heavens to study the skies—you have the power to do all this, but you cannot change the fact, nor the truth of the fact, by one jot. (*Stamping the earth with his foot.*) It moves!!

MARIA CELESTE. "Hear my prayer, Oh Lord, and let my cry come unto Thee. For I am clean forgotten, as a dead man out of mind. I am become like a broken vessel. My days are consumed away like smoke; and my bones are burnt up as a firebrand. My heart is tormented. My eyes are destroyed out of grief, the light

100

is gone from them. My days are gone like a shadow. Deliver my soul, Oh Lord, save me for Thy mercy's sake. Glory be to the Father, and to the Son, and to the Holy Ghost, world without end. Amen."

GALILEO. Where is the meeting ground between faith and reason? Or, is the human mind incapable of operating in the realm of religion and must therefore humbly accept revealed truth on faith alone and with no understanding? If so, what of knowledge derived from experience? I say that if a man takes away reason to make room for revelation he puts out the light of both. Help me, Oh God. Give me a measure for the truth! . . . It does move!

MARIA CELESTE. "Out of the deep have I called unto Thee, Oh Lord, Lord, hear my voice. Hear my prayer, Oh Lord, my heart within me is desolate. Hide not Thy face from me, lest I be like those who go down into the pit. Show me the way that I should walk in, for I lift up my soul unto Thee. Teach me to do the thing that pleaseth Thee, for Thou art my God; let Thy loving Spirit lead me forth."

GALILEO. Is Polissena right? Can I earn the worth of my days through work? Search for the laws of force and motion? "Make a sword of your sorrow." Will work forge this sword? Can I earn my redemption? . . . I swear by my Lord and Saviour, the earth does move!! (*The lights have been dimming down. Now there is a*)

BLACKOUT

THE END

A PILGRIM POOR

Adapted from Early 17th Century
Songs by Barrie Stavis
Lyrics by Barrie Stavis

In quick tempo

A pil-grim poor to Zi-ta came one day, and
for a lit-tle wa-ter he did pray. "I wish, my
broth-er, I could give thee wine, but if the wa-ter please
thee, that is thine!" This said, she drew the wa-
ter from the well and with a cross the pitch-er did
she sign. "Oh Lord" she said, while low her sweet
voice fell, "Make Thou this wa-ter sweet for one of
Thine." The pil-grim drank, then as-ton-ished raised his
head, "But tru-ly this is pre-cious wine," he said.

OH, DARKENED HOUSE

Adapted from Early 17th Century
Songs by Barrie Stavis
Lyrics by Barrie Stavis

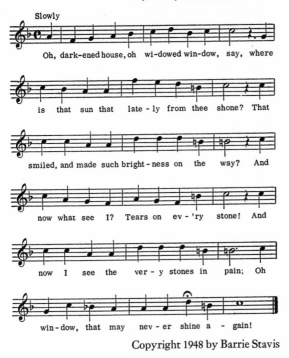

Oh, dark-ened house, oh wi-dowed win-dow, say, where is that sun that late-ly from thee shone? That smiled, and made such bright-ness on the way? And now what see I? Tears on ev-'ry stone! And now I see the ver-y stones in pain; Oh win-dow, that may nev-er shine a - gain!

103

Doubling Suggestions

CHARACTER	CAN PLAY IN
Gepe	any scene after Act II, Scene 1
Sagredo	any scene in Act III
Magini, Sizzi, D'Elci and Libri	any scene after Act I, Scene 2
Cesi	any scene in Acts II and III
All Lynx Members (except Maffeo Barberini)	any scene in Acts II and III
Viesta, Viglienna, Naples and Father Clavius	any scene in Acts II and III
Cardinals Zacchia and Verospi	any scene in Act II
Bellarmin	any scene in Acts II and III
Venetti, Landini and Page	any scene in Acts I and III
Carlo and Francesco	any scene in Act I
Major Domo, Riccardi, Ciampoli and Two Soldiers	any scene in Acts I and III
Firenzuola	any scene in Act I
Clerk, Inquisitors, Dominicans, and all Cardinals except Zacchia and Verospi	any scene in Acts I and II

Characters Who Can Be Eliminated If Necessary

1. Several of the Lynx Members; speeches can be run together as needed.

2. In Act I, Scene 4, Cardinal Bellarmin can address one Father instead of four.

3. Only one Soldier can be used in Act II, Scene 6.

4. In the Inquisition Scene, Act III, Scene I, only one Inquisitor besides Firenzuola can be used, and one Dominican who can also act as Clerk.

5. The number of Cardinals in Act III, Scene 3, can be reduced to eight.

Pronunciation of Names

GALILEO GALILEI	gal-i-lay'-o ga-li-lay'-ee
POLISSENA	po-lis-sa'-na
(later SISTER	
MARIA CELESTE)	ma-ree-a cha-lest'
SAGREDO NICCOLINI	sa-gray'-do nek-ko-lee'-nee
GEPE MAZZOLINI	dje-pe mat-so-lee'-nee
MAGINI	ma-djee'-nee
SIZZI	seet'-see
LIBRI	lee'-bree
D'ELCI	del'-chee
CESI	chay'-see
FABRICIUS	fa-brish'-us
TERENZIO	te-ren'-zio
CESARE	cha'-sa-ree
MOROSINI	mo-ro-see'-nee
ZACCHIA	zock'-ea
MAFFEO BARBERINI	ma-fe'-o bar-be-ree'-nee
ALDOBRANDINI	al-do-bran-dee'-nee
VIESTA	ve-est'-a
VIGLIENNA	vil-yen'-a
BELLARMIN	bel'-ar-min
CLAVIUS	clav'-ius
VEROSPI	ve-ros'-pee
CARLO	car'-lo
FRANCESCO	fran-ches'-ko
VENETTI	ve-net'-tee
LANDINI	lan-dee'-nee
FIRENZUOLA	fee-ren-zoo-o'-la
RICCARDI	ree-kar'-dee
CIAMPOLI	cham-po'-lee
BORGIA	bor'-dja
ARCETRI	ar-cha'-tree

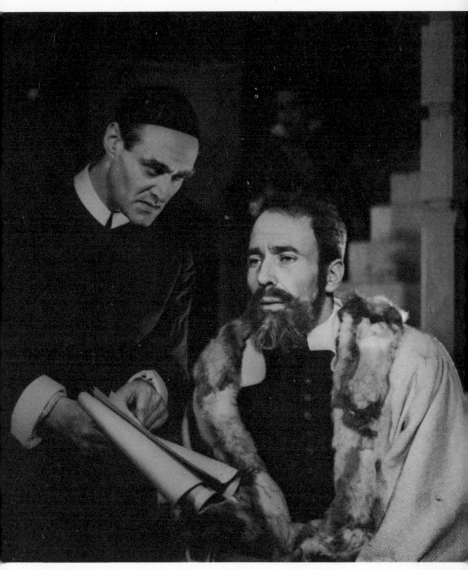

New Stages, Inc., production, December 21, 1947, New
York. (Paul Mann, left, and Peter Capell)

Amherst College production, January 1948. (Robert Brustein, left, as Firenzuola, and Donald V. Roberts as Galileo)

Bristol Old Vic production, October 16, 1956. (Peter O'Toole, second from left, as Pope Urban VIII. Photo by Desmond Tripp)

Brigham Young University production, January 1965.

List of Properties

ACT	SCENE	
1	1	Breakaway telescope, consisting of lens, lens holder, barrel (tube) and stand
		Polishing cloth, dish of food, charts, dividers, inkwell, letter, quill, lute
1	2	Large book, small book, charts, telescope, handkerchief
1	3	Goblets, Book of Lynx Members, inkwell, quill, list of names
1	4	Four telescopes
1	5	Memorandum
1	6	No props
2	1	Wrapped telescope, bowl of food, medicine bottle, jar of salve, manuscript
2	2	Gifts, letter, ring
2	3	Several books, a coin, letter
2	4	Two books, memorandum
2	5	No props
2	6	No props
3	1	Quills, papers, Bible, crucifix, inkwell, file of papers, book
3	2	Paper
3	3	Inkwells, quills, document
3	4	Bible, quill, inkwell, document
3	5	Lute, letters, book, rose